THE
DECOY DUCK

FROM FOLK ART TO FINE ART

THE
DECOY DUCK
FROM FOLK ART TO FINE ART

Bob Ridges

B. Mitchell

ACKNOWLEDGEMENTS

I am deeply indebted to the many decoy carvers and collectors who co-operated with me to make this book possible, also to the museum curators who allowed me to photograph their decoy collections. In one or two instances I have used illustrations where I have been unable to make the usual acknowledgement in the picture credits to the carver concerned, simply because I was unable to trace them. For this I apologise and hope that they will excuse me.

This book would not have been possible without the support and co-operation of my dear wife Sophie, who 'held the fort' while I was travelling in America and generally aided and abetted the whole project in countless ways.

Finally, I have to thank the thousands of people who during recent years have responded so enthusiastically to my work and thus made it possible for me to earn a living doing what I enjoy best in life – carving ducks.

Dragon's World Ltd
High Street
Limpsfield
Surrey RH8 0DY
Great Britain

ISBN 0 88665 482 3

CONTENTS

INTRODUCTION

Head detail of Pintail drake by Curt Fabre

Ruddy duck by Mark McNair

The genesis of the art of decorative decoy carving is a uniquely American phenomenon. It was inspired by, and evolved directly from, the floating wooden decoys used by hunters to bring wildfowl within range of their weapons.

These same hunting decoys, which were made as practical artefacts or tools of the hunt, have themselves now become recognised as folk art and are avidly collected by people often prepared to pay huge sums of money for them.

Interest in the subject has become widespread not only across America, where it all began, but now increasingly around the world where more and more people are beginning to carve and collect decoys.

It is my aim in this book to provide a broad overview of the subject for the reader who may have recently become interested in decoys. Such a person will have many questions to ask and it is hoped that the answers to many of them will be found within these pages. For in-depth study, there are many fine books available and these will be referred to wherever they are considered helpful.

Since I first became interested in decoys and decoy carving in the late 1970s I have travelled to many of the areas where decoy history was made and have been fortunate enough to meet many interesting people who have been good enough to share with me their knowledge and interest in the subject. I hope that in turn I can share with the reader some of the discoveries and excitement of my quest.

Photography, for the most part, was done 'on the spot' with basic camera equipment and relying very much on the automatic mode of the camera, a Canon AE 1.

The carver artists featured in these pages are really a random selection, representative of the whole. Some are world champions, some hobby carvers, some have spent a lifetime making decoys, some have been carving for barely a year. There are many top class carvers whose work has not been included – there simply wasn't space for everyone. I felt it was important to show something of the diversity of carving styles and to indicate the vigorous growth of the art form and its appeal to a wide cross-section of people.

DEFINITIONS

In order to be able to understand the narrative fully, it is necessary to define several terms which will appear frequently in the text.

Decoy

An artefact used by hunters to lure wildfowl or fish within range of their weapons. Also referred to as 'gunning decoy', 'gunner', 'stool', 'block', 'working decoy'.

The usual collective noun for a group of decoys used for hunting is a 'rig'.

Canada goose decoys. Refuge Waterfowl Museum, Chincoteague

Bluejay exhibited at the Easton Waterfowl Festival

Decorative decoy

A bird or fish carving, possibly capable of being used as a working decoy but really intended as a decorative object to be enjoyed as art.

In this category there may be two styles of carving:

(1) 'Decoy Style' decorative where the carver intends the finished work to evoke the spirit and form of the hunting decoy, even though the piece is clearly decorative.

(2) 'Realistic Style' decorative where the carver aims to produce a painted carving as close to nature as possible. It will almost certainly be 'feather textured' (or in the case of a fish have textured scales). If it is not feather textured, it is called a 'slick'.

Confidence decoy

A working decoy added to a hunter's rig to inspire confidence in the quarry. Gulls and herons in particular make useful confidence decoys, both being wary birds which would spook at the first sign of danger.

Stick-ups

Flat board cutouts of ducks and geese mounted on a spike and set out in fields or marsh as decoys.

Shorebird decoys

Decoys designed to lure the birds that frequent the seashore, e.g., yellowlegs, dowitchers, curlews. These decoys were set on a stick which was pushed into the ground. They are sometimes simply referred to as 'snipe decoys'.

ORIGINS

The mouth of the SE Pipe from the pond

Man has always been a hunter and has exploited every conceivable ploy to trap, snare and lure his quarry. The first requirement of any successful hunter is to observe his quarry closely in order to learn its migrations, its habits and the way it thinks so that he can anticipate how it will react in every situation. If he can find certain predictable traits that can be exploited, he greatly improves the chances of succeeding in his hunt.

One of the first things a wildfowl hunter notes about wildfowl is their tendency to flock together, to fly in to join other resting, feeding and apparently secure birds on the water. To exploit this predictable behaviour the hunter has several options and these have been used in different ways around the world, depending very much upon the particular conditions and circumstances in which the hunter found himself.

The word decoy derives from the Dutch 'de kooi' meaning 'the cage (or trap)' or possibly from 'eende kooi' meaning 'duck cage (or trap)'. It relates to an ingenious and effective method of harvesting wildfowl employed in Holland and first recorded in the seventeenth century. The method was introduced to Britain by Dutch drainage engineers employed to drain part of the Fens, the great marshes of East Anglia, around 1650. One such decoy still exists at Borough Fen, in Cambridgeshire, a few miles north of Peterborough. It is remarkable on several counts. Firstly, it has been in continuous use since 1670 when it was established by the Earl of Lincoln and secondly, it was operated down the centuries by decoymen from one family – the Williams family. Sadly that line ended in 1958 with the death of Billy Williams. He was survived by his widow, Annie Williams, who died in January 1987, at the age of 97. I had the pleasure of meeting this fine old lady about a year before her death. Her body may have been frail but her mind was as clear as a girl's, and she was able to tell me how she helped her husband operate the decoy and something of their life and times.

Borough Fen Decoy is set in flat open farmland and consists of a two and a half acre pond surrounded by fourteen and a half acres of woodland. It is a silent, almost secret place, the only sounds being the gentle sough of the wind in the trees and the occasional strident quack of a mallard duck on the pond. Eight

CHARLES R.—The Workes and Services comprised in this Account, were done by our direction, May 30, 1671.

To Edward Maybank and Tho. Greene for digging the Decoy and carrying out the earth and levelling the ground about the said Decoy 128 2 11½
To Edward Storey [1] for wyer and other things used about the Decoy, and for 100 Baskets for the Ducks . . . 8 9 0
To Oliver Honey for paving the feeding place for the Ducks and breaking the ground 1 10 0
To Sr George Waterman for several Netts for the Decoy . 15 3 0
To Edward Storey for money paid to sundry workmen for setting the Reeds and Polles round the Decoy and wyering it 9 10 0
To John Scott for Carpenter's Worke done in Wharfing and making Bridges in the Island and Borders, and for Boards used about the Decoy and other Work . . . 45 15 4

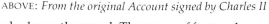
ABOVE: *From the original Account signed by Charles II*

Tony Cook rings a Mallard drake caught in the decoy

curving 'pipes' radiate from the pond, each one covered by netted hoops narrowing to a tunnel in which the duck would be driven and caught. An elaborate arrangement of screens and low 'dog leaps' along each pipe, conceals the decoyman from the ducks on the pond and enables him to work the dog to draw the ducks into the pipe. The dog, which by tradition has tended to be small and fox-like and invariably called 'Piper', is trained to appear from behind the screens in view of the ducks on the water and then to disappear from sight behind the next. This arouses the curiosity of the ducks which swim in towards the pipe to investigate. This process is repeated progressively from screen to screen down the pipe until the ducks are sufficiently within the pipe cage. They can then be driven by the decoyman, who can now appear through the intriguingly-called 'yackoop' – a gap in the screen – to drive the ducks down the pipe. To aid the process, grain and potatoes could be used to bait the pipe and sometimes live decoy ducks, noted for their loud quacking call, were used to lure the wild ducks on the pond to their fate. Since much of the work might be done in the half light of dawn or dusk, white decoy ducks were preferred as there was less chance of them having their necks wrung by mistake.

Eight pipes were necessary to allow the decoyman to be always downwind of his quarry and, of course, absolute silence had to be observed to avoid spooking the ducks on the pond. The maze of footpaths around the pipes had to be kept soft underfoot with sawdust – even a snapping twig could give the game away. The harvesting of wildfowl in this way was a serious business: the decoymen took great pride in their skill and sent impressive quantities of birds to the profitable markets in London.

This ancient decoy is now operated by The Wildfowl Trust at Peakirk a few miles away. Its curator, Tony Cook, knew and worked with Billy Williams and has spent almost a quarter of a century operating the decoy. Since 1954 the slaughter of ducks for market has ceased and wild birds are now caught only to be ringed and recorded for scientific purposes.*

Such decoys existed in other parts of Britain. Indeed, in St James's Park in central London there was a place known as the King's Decoy, established by Charles II in 1671 – no doubt a source of succulent wild duck for the Royal table.

I recently discovered a place called Decoy Farm on the ancient marsh known as the Somerset Levels not far from my home in the Mendip Hills, but there is no remaining evidence of a decoy there, other than the name.

From the wall paintings left by the ancient Egyptians we know that noblemen wildfowlers used live tethered duck to attract wild duck. This method works well, although there are obvious disadvantages, overcome in the case of the Egyptian noblemen by having a large retinue of servants to handle the live decoys. This method was certainly used to some extent in America within the living memory of people I have spoken with. The use of live decoys was, however, banned in America in 1934.

Long before white settlers landed in the vast silent continent of North America, American Indian hunters had perfected special skills in hunting wildfowl. In a remarkable find at Lovelock Cave in Nevada in 1924, archaeologists found 11 very well preserved American Indian Canvasback decoys. They were made of reeds bound together in the shape of the floating bird and covered in a skin of the bird with feathers to add realism. They were complete with anchor tethers and it was clear how they were deployed for hunting. These relics were dated at

The History of Borough Fen Decoy by T. Cook and R.E.M. Pilcher.

RIGHT: *Tony Cook with 'Piper' at the end of the pipe*

BELOW: *'Piper' being deployed behind the screens. Note fox-like appearance of the dog*

BOTTOM: *The curving pipe showing the staggered screens with 'dog leaps' between*

more than 1,000 years old. We shall never know whether they were part of a burial ritual, intended for use in the great wildfowl hunt beyond the grave or simply left there by a hunter who meant to pick them up later but for whatever reason did not return. These relics are now preserved in the Museum of the American Indian in New York.

At around the time when the word 'decoy' was first being used in the English language, English settlers were struggling to establish themselves in settlements on the American East coast. The early years before crops could be established were harsh, and many died of hunger and disease. History records much friendly co-operation between the local native Indians and settlers in both New England and at Jamestown, Virginia. The settlers who survived

Decoy duck of tule rush, covered with feathers. Courtesy of Museum of the American Indian, Heye Foundation, N.Y.

*M. R. Harrington with duck decoys of tule rush covered
with feathers, as found.
Courtesy of Museum of the American Indian, Heye
Foundation, N.Y.*

probably owed their lives to the fact that joint hunting parties obtained food, the Indians providing local knowledge and hunting skills and the white man firearms. It is almost certain that the early settlers learned of the use of floating decoys from the Indians and, having better tools, started to fashion decoys from wood.

There is no evidence of the European method of decoying ever becoming established in the New World, and the reason would appear to be the abundance of wildfowl in America and the ease with which they could be hunted. All the hunter had to do was bring the flocks of ducks and geese into his decoys and the rest was simple. From the very beginning, hunting in America was part of survival and any man was free to go out into marsh or river and hunt food for his table. This differed greatly from the situation in Europe where generally the common man had no hunting rights over land held by powerful landowners.

Halfway through the nineteenth century several factors led to what has been described as the greatest hunt in the history of the world'. The old muzzle loading rifle, clumsy and slow for hunting, gave way to the far more efficient breach loader which, with better ammunition and speedier action, improved the hunter's efficiency. America was booming; railways were opening up the country and its vast resources, immigrants were pouring in from Europe, and the cities were growing rapidly. The hotels and restaurants of Boston, New York, Philadelphia and Baltimore were willing to pay good prices for seafood and succulent wildfowl. Anyone who could get his kill quickly to a railway was assured of a ready market. This gave rise to the era of 'market hunting' when professional hunters blazed away at the seemingly inexhaustible flights of ducks and geese that filled the skies along the Eastern seaboard of America. Their kills often ran into hundreds of swans, geese and duck in a single day and they used vast rigs of decoys on a similar scale. Some gunners set out rigs of several hundred decoys, often using a sink box as a floating hide in the middle of the decoys. This low freeboard vessel had outboards on which were set heavy cast iron decoys to help keep the sink box low in the water. These had sometimes to be jettisoned if the water became rough and threatened to swamp the sink box. Other rigs would be set out from a convenient point of land on which the hunter could build a hide.

The market hunters made their own decoys or bought them from professional decoy makers who turned out sturdy workaday birds that had to stand up to the rigours of wind and weather and rough handling. At this time the only criteria of a decoy were that it was durable, effective and cheap. Some of the finest decoys ever made were produced during this era, yet whilst a particular maker's decoy might be admired, it was not usually judged from the standpoint of artistic merit but simply by those three criteria. The days of artistic recognition were yet to dawn.

This wholesale slaughter of wildfowl eventually caused trouble. A number of species of duck became scarce, the Labrador duck became extinct and several other hunted birds, notably the passenger pigeon, were being wiped out for ever. Public concern resulted in Congress passing the Migratory Bird Act in 1918. This effectively put an end to 'market hunting' which had flourished for nearly 70 years. When the end came, the market hunters put away their guns and turned to other ways of making a living. It is easy to look back on the 'market hunters' and think of them as ignorant, greedy, bloodthirsty men who had no thought for the consequences of their actions. In the main they were no worse and no better than any other of their contemporaries. Generally they were fishermen and farmers who saw an opportunity and did what they did as well as they could.

For some of the full-time decoy makers these were difficult times. Apart from the making of new decoys, there had always been maintenance work and re-painting of old decoys to keep them busy. Once this fell away they were in much the same position as the farrier when the motor car replaced horses as transport.

The decoys themselves often lay around for years before being burned as firewood, or left rotting on the foreshore. Some decoys were used by hunters to put food on their own tables and 'sports' came down from the cities to hunt for pleasure. During the Depression years many people hunted to survive, weighing the cost of each cartridge against the chance of a duck or goose for the table. This brought something of a revival in decoy making.

BASICS

*Rig of 'Cigar' Daisey decoys at the Refuge Waterfowl
Museum, Chincoteague*

Decoys come in all shapes and sizes, styles and forms. In the right conditions wild-fowl will decoy to plastic containers set out on the water. Red Indian hunters are said to place one small round pebble on top of another larger round pebble to make a duck look-alike on the shore. Generally, decoys were made from whatever came cheaply and easily to hand and their design and style was dictated by the conditions they would encounter in use. A spar from a wrecked ship could provide a dozen or more decoys, as could old telegraph poles or timbers from an old barn. With saw and hand axe, draw knife and spokeshave, decoys were usually quickly and crudely made. It was sufficient that when the rig was set out in front of a blind that it pulled the birds. Painting was likewise usually quite rudimentary; ordinary house paints and paint used for fishing boats was thinned down with a little petrol to 'flatten' it and take away the gloss. Gloss paint might cause a decoy to shine and spook the birds. Another way to avoid a shiny paint finish was to paint in the evening and leave the bird to dry in the open over-night. The damp dewy conditions would then remove the gloss.

A floating decoy has to be weighted so that it will ride upright in the water, and if thrown from a boat will right itself naturally. Most makers cast their own weights, often in distinctive shapes, which some-times gives a useful clue to the maker's identity if the origin of a decoy is in question. Other forms of weight were used, such as old horseshoes and pieces of chain.

The decoy has also to be anchored and will have an attachment for the anchor line. If it has a keel, then there will be a hole through which the anchor line is attached. If there is no keel, there is likely to be a leather loop for the anchor line or perhaps a metal ring and staple. Anchors are usually of lead and come in a wide variety of shapes and styles deter-mined by the nature of the bottom where the decoys are used. In muddy conditions an anchor has to stick well into the holding ground, in rocky ground the anchor has to be designed to avoid snagging. Some decoy anchors were made of cast steel and sold by sporting goods stores – I have heard these referred to as 'rich boy' anchors. Collecting decoy anchors is a growing interest, and as these can often be picked up for just a few dollars they are worth looking out for.

Decoys often have a brand stamped on the bottom, usually the initials of the carver or owner. When a hunter owned a large rig of maybe several hundred decoys, he needed to be able to prove ownership if decoys broke loose in a storm – a quite frequent occurrence.

In some regions decoys were hollowed to make them lighter and therefore easier to carry, to give them added buoyancy and to make them float with the lightness of a duck on the water. The so-called 'New Jersey Dugout' decoy is a good example. Another advantage of hollowing a decoy is that the wood tends to be more stable as a result: solid wood tends to 'check' – to split and open. A hollow decoy feels good; its lightness is pleasing. Often the maker leaves a chip of wood inside to let you know it is hollow if you shake the bird. Some decoys from Louisiana made from cypress root are so light that they seem to be hollow.

An expert can usually tell at a glance where a decoy was made. The local conditions in which a decoy was used determined to a large extent its characteristics. Some decoys were likely to be deployed in rough open water where they had to ride well and be seen in the chop. This called for a robust decoy often larger in size than the live bird. By contrast decoys used on the sheltered bayous and swamps of Louisiana tended to be neat and much nearer to life size.

In most areas there appears to be a predominant maker who hit upon a design which was effective and ideal in the prevailing conditions. This design was copied by contemporaries and others who fol-lowed. There is no suggestion here of plagiarism. Remember we are not yet talking of art. In what were often tightly-knit communities, decoy makers were almost certain to know each other, indeed they were more than likely to be good friends. Given the interest that decoys and hunting generate, a great deal of visiting and yarning took place. There is no place in the world so cosy as a decoy carver's work-shop on a winter's evening with the pot-bellied stove giving off a good heat, the marvellous smell of cedar and pine and maybe a beer or two or something stronger to get people talking. Visitors will always pick up the latest piece being worked on and cast a critical eye over it. If what they see pleases them, you

may be sure they will try something similar themselves soon. Discussion can range almost endlessly about the number of birds or lack of them, the shots that missed and the composition of the rig. A rig might include decoys representing a number of species. If canvasback were the main quarry, then the rig might well include a majority of canvasback decoys with a few swans, a few teal or wigeon or whatever. If a particular formula worked well it would be used until things went wrong and then adjustments would be made to try to restore good results. Each hunter had his own ideas on what constituted a perfect rig and much debating, trading and swopping of decoys took place in the quest for the perfect formula. Among friends patterns were freely exchanged and over time these were considered almost common property. A Havre de Grace maker today makes Havre de Grace style decoys of a style and pattern that have always been made in that area. Although this gives decoys a recognisable regional identity, makers imparted to their birds their own stamp of individuality which makes them easily distinguishable to a trained eye.

Inevitably, there were among decoy makers individuals who brought to their work a quality which made it stand out as something special. Decoy makers as a whole knew their wildfowl. Most of them hunted and were keen observers of the birds they hunted. Most were appreciative of the beauty and elegance of their subject. Those with artistic ability strove to capture the finest essence of the subject bird, both in the carving and in the painting. They were constrained by the requirements of a hunting decoy to be practical and robust, yet they always strove to improve the shape and lifelike quality of their decoys.

There are really three critical stages in making a fine decoy. Firstly there is the pattern. The pattern represents all the keen observation of the subject set out in two of its three dimensions, if the shape is first cut on a bandsaw. The carving of the third dimension is the second stage. Here the carver's mastery of his tools and the wood and his eye for the final shape determines the quality of his product. Even without paint there will be no doubt as to the identity of the subject bird. The third and final stage of painting the wood will be the final embellishment. If done well it will bring the bird to life.

To the enthusiast most decoys are appealing but a really fine example by one of the great master decoy makers, such as Shang Wheeler, Joe Lincoln, A. Elmer Crowell, Charles Walker, the Ward brothers, William Bowman and William Shourds, have a quality that sets them apart as something special. Among decoy collectors and enthusiasts they evoke the same sort of reverence as the work of any great artist or craftsman.

In 1934 the book *Wild Fowl Decoys* by Joel Barber was published in America. It drew attention to the merit of bird decoys and the delights of collecting them. Barber attempted to record something of the history of decoys and their makers and he did so with a romantic appreciation of the subject which opened many people's eyes to the fascination not only of the decoys themselves but also of the lives and times of the men who carved them. Barber was an architect, an urbane, educated man, and he brought an aesthetic appreciation to the subject. He made accurate drawings and watercolours of decoys that appealed to him. It was Barber who coined the term 'floating sculpture', attributing to decoys, perhaps for the first time, artistic merit that had until then been overlooked. It is interesting to note that in his book, although Barber attributes aesthetic merit to the subject, all the decoys reviewed and illustrated are working decoys, that is, made to be hunted over. The day of the decorative decoy was about to dawn.

Classic Shorebird decoy by William Bowman
By courtesy of the Shelburne Museum

THE WARD BROTHERS

Lem and Steve Ward. Photo by Aubrey Bodine. By courtesy of Jack R. Schroeder

The Eastern Shore of the Chesapeake (often referred to as the Delmarva peninsula because it is comprised of parts of the three states DELaware, MARyland and VirginiA) is bordered on its east side by the Atlantic Ocean and on the west by the rich waters of the Chesapeake Bay.

The bay has always provided a rich harvest of crabs, oysters and fish. The low flat land of 'the shore' provides not only rich farmland and forest but its plentiful rivers, inlets and marshes make it an ideal habitat for the duck, swans and geese that winter on the shore each year.

The shore was settled in the mid-seventeenth century by settlers of mainly English stock, evidenced by such place names as Oxford and Cambridge, Dover and Salisbury. There are many American Indian names, mostly of rivers and islands, to remind us of the original inhabitants of this place.

This Ward Brothers Canada goose has been adopted as the symbol of the Ward Foundation. It represents their work at its finest and is on display at the North American Wildfowl Art Museum, Salisbury, Maryland. Photo by the author. By courtesy of the Ward Foundation

It is generally agreed that the birthplace of decorative decoy carving was the small town of Crisfield, situated on the bayside of the Eastern shore. In the boom days of the market hunting era, Crisfield was a bustling, prosperous place. Regular ferry services linked it with the mainland and large quantities of valuable fish, oysters, crabs and wildfowl were shipped out daily. The inhabitants of the town were nearly all connected with the water, either as fishermen or boatmen. They lived to the rhythm of the tides and seasons and the migration of the wildfowl and although life might at times be hard, when winter gales whipped up the waters of the bay into a fury, for most it was a healthy open-air life close to nature.

Two brothers, Lem and Steve Ward, were part of this community. They lived 'down neck', the poorer part of town. They ran a small barber shop and they carved decoys. Steve (1895–1976) was a strong healthy man who in his youth had been an amateur

*Lem Ward in workshop, 1977. By courtesy of the
Ward Foundation*

boxer. In the War he served his country as far afield as France. His brother Lem (1896–1984) was born virtually a cripple and so frail in health that it was thought he would not survive to reach manhood. Yet somehow he did and lived to be a good age.

The brothers enjoyed a close relationship and were popular in the community. They were part of a barber shop harmony singing group and loved listening to baseball on the radio. They were God-fearing, generous to a degree and would go out of their way to do a kindness if they could. Steve enjoyed writing poetry, Lem was a gifted natural artist.

Wildfowl hunting was a natural part of life on the Eastern shore. There were gunning clubs which provided for visiting sportsmen – known locally as 'sports' – who came to the shore to shoot wildfowl. They needed decoys and the Wards supplied their needs and repaired and repainted the decoys as required. Steve made his first decoy in 1907 and Lem

his first in 1918. Customers coming to the barber shop didn't seem to mind the woodshavings on the floor; indeed they probably took a keen interest in the fine duck and goose decoys that the brothers made.

The depression years of the 1930s made life difficult for everyone in Crisfield. Without work it was often necessary to turn to the marshes to find a meal for the table. Steve and Lem made good decoys and sold them for a mere dollar or two, often allowing the price of a decoy and a haircut to go 'on the slate' to help those who were hard up.

In time, word of the quality of Ward decoys spread. Visiting sportsmen started to come by the small workshop. These customers had money. There were doctors and lawyers, industrialists and senators. The brothers found that clients were buying their work not just to shoot over but to adorn mantelpieces and studies. They also found that birds with a little extra

Ward decoys in the collection of Dr Morton and Carol Kramer

detail, perhaps a turned head or a raised wing and a bit of detailed painting, were soon snapped up by these collectors.

This was fine. Nothing appealed to the brothers more than to give free rein to the latent artistry they possessed in such abundance. Eventually, but not without considerable deliberation, – for in an uncertain world cutting hair represented a reliable trade – they closed the barber shop business. The old barber shop was moved back and attached to the decoy workshop, to produce a larger, somewhat odd-looking building which nevertheless served its purpose. Their rate of production was now considerable. They made delightful half-size miniatures and these sold like hot cakes. They worked not to make money so much as to do something they enjoyed doing as well as they could. In a sense they were already rich, having everything they needed. They never owned a car – they didn't need one. A bicycle got them around town and down to the waterfront. Any money that did come their way was used to improve the family home or was given away to family or friends who might be in need.

By the late 1940s the Ward brothers were well known. They had won prizes with their work at Decoy Shows in New York and more and more collectors beat a path to their door. Decoys had now become recognised as a uniquely American folk art and collecting was becoming quite fashionable, even if still on a very small scale. At this time the Wards were directing most of their efforts towards ornamental carvings. This could not have been better as hunting around Crisfield was in decline and Canvasbacks, the premium hunting duck of this area, were becoming so scarce that hunting them was eventually banned in 1959.

A feature of the Wards' work was the constant experimenting with the patterns and designs of their decoys. Many makers stayed with the same patterns, often the traditional patterns of the locality, and produced these standard decoys throughout their career. The Wards, especially Lem who was the artist, enjoyed trying new shapes, always moving towards perfection. There was constantly something new going on in their workshop and this was a great attraction. Sometimes they found it hard to get on with their work because they had so many visitors. Then they would put up a sign, 'Closed for

Ward Brothers Canvasback drake decoy

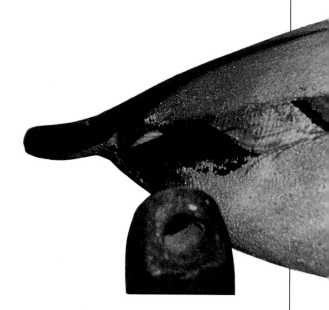

business!' But they enjoyed meeting people and their friendship was highly valued in return. Although not well educated, they wrote letters expressing their friendship, sometimes accompanied by a poem they had written. They especially enjoyed making a decoy for a good friend, often writing a special message on the underside of the bird.

A typical Ward brothers decoy had a finely stylised form with clean lines which invariably captured the essence of the bird to perfection. It might be made from a variety of woods; they used pretty much anything that came to hand – even balsa wood taken from Second World War life rafts, washed up on the

shore. Balsa decoys worked well but tended to absorb water quite quickly unless they were sealed thoroughly before painting. Old telegraph poles of cedar cypress or juniper were used and white cedar, white pine and basswood whenever they could get it.

Many of their early decoys were solid but as this caused problems with checking, they later hollowed out their birds to stabilise the wood.

They used a large old-fashioned bandsaw to cut out the basic shape of their decoys, then they would use a hand axe and drawknife to round the body, finishing with a spokeshave. They also had a belt sander with a six-inch wide belt. By twisting a spiral into the belt they could achieve the fine, curved shapes which gave their birds such style. The bird was then hand sanded before painting. Steve did most of the carving.

Lem handled the painting and over the years developed a highly distinctive style which makes Ward decoys unique. In the early days he followed traditional Crisfield paint patterns – their father Travis Ward had been a decoy maker before them, so they had grown up in the tradition – gradually developing his own refinements as time went by.

After first priming with a standard wood primer – Lem preferred a brand called Furzite – the rest of the

Oliver Lawson

painting was done with artist's oil, using good quality artist's brushes. Various stippling techniques achieved fine feather effects and subtlety of colour blending. Even with their hunting decoys, painting was never hurried; the brothers always strove for perfection. They enjoyed their work and took pleasure from doing the best they could. They were inspired by a love of nature and marvelled at the beauty of God's creation. Quite simply they sought to reflect that beauty in their work.

As the Ward decorative carvings became better known through exhibitions and magazine articles, they inspired a new generation of carvers who carried on the impetus of this exciting new art form as the Wards grew older.

Among the young carvers, on whom the Wards had great influence, were two Crisfield boys, Oliver Lawson and Don Briddell.

Lawson lived two miles from the Wards' workshop. His mother worked for a time with Lem's wife, Thelma, and when he was ten years old young Oliver was invited into the workshop to see what was going on. Noting his great interest, Steve and Lem encouraged the boy to try carving. He showed an immediate aptitude and soon he was racing home from school each day to go down to the workshop where he was allowed to help. Like most youngsters in Crisfield, Lawson couldn't wait to be old enough to have a gun and go hunting. To hunt you needed decoys and his first priority was to make his own rig.

But soon this remarkable young man was displaying an uncanny ability both as a carver and painter. He absorbed everything he could in the Wards' workshop. Out in the marshes he hunted ducks and closely observed their habits and flight, their colours and form. At first he carved just as a hobby but in due course collectors started to take an interest in his work and commissions began coming in.

In 1965 he entered his first show and competition where he did well. Although he strove for perfection, competitions did not greatly appeal to him and generally he preferred to work quietly on his own. His work continued to improve and it became clear that he could make a living as a carver doing the work he enjoyed most. Today much of his work still shows a strong Ward influence, which Lawson is happy to acknowledge. He has been an innovative artist who has tried many new techniques and was one of the

Ward style Canvasback hen by Oliver Lawson

Red Breasted Merganser by Oliver Lawson
By courtesy of the Refuge Waterfowl Museum, Chincoteague

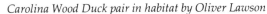

Carolina Wood Duck pair in habitat by Oliver Lawson

first to do decorative 'set piece' carvings, depicting birds in their natural habitat. His fine carving of a pair of Carolina Wood Ducks is an excellent example of this kind of work.

Don Briddell also grew up in Crisfield. He was a classmate of Lem's grandson Tommy and he was also invited into the Ward workshop. There he was given his first block and instructions on how to carve a decoy. Soon he too found himself carving every spare minute, even getting in an hour before school. Briddell remembers how the Wards helped him. 'They always praised and encouraged, were ever ready to offer patient, helpful advice. Their tools

were quite poor compared to what we have today. Lem used a cheap "chicken pickin" knife someone gave him, to do the fine carving on his birds. He didn't complain and it seemed to work well for him.'

He remembers, too, the warm hospitality. 'They were poor but if you were there at a meal time there was always an extra place for you at table.'

Of the brothers he said, 'They were like night and day – completely complementary to each other – two sides of the same coin.'

One day the millionaire industrialist Du Pont, an avid hunter, came by the Ward shop and commissioned Lem to make a complete set of native

Detail of Carolina Wood Duck carving by Oliver Lawson

Don Briddell

Mallard hen by Don Briddell

American waterfowl. A price was negotiated that seemed in total to add up to more money than there was likely to be in the whole world – by their standards. Briddell laughs as he recalls, 'They were so amazed at the length of his Cadillac, they figured it must have a hinge in the middle to get around corners.'

Lem made only 16 pieces of the commission before he was crippled by a stroke which left him unable to carve ever again.

As Briddell grew up his interest in wildfowl carving became secondary to a longing to have a driving licence. A 'hot rod' car became the great love of his life and he had ambitions to design cars for General Motors. With this end in view he left Crisfield to attend the famous Pratt Institute of Design in Brooklyn. Carving now became a holiday activity only, to make a little extra money to indulge his passion for cars.

On graduation Don's life took a new direction. He joined the Peace Corps, and travelled widely overseas for ten years.

When he returned to Crisfield he found that much had happened on the carving scene during his absence. He saw the direction Lem's work had taken and found himself once again inspired to take up his knife and paintbrush. By now regular competitions were being held and he entered these and did well. Again, like Lawson and perhaps because of the Ward influence, he found competitions not entirely to his liking. He recognised that they were valuable in stimulating carvers to raise their standards but still preferred to go his own way. 'For many people winning blue ribbons was all that mattered and some of the collectors, too, cared only about blue ribbon pieces.'

Don Briddell returned full time to being a decorative decoy carver and today his work is recognised for its fine quality by collectors around the world. The Ward influence can be seen, too, in his work. He has spent a great deal of time cataloguing their patterns and recording as much information as possible about these two men whose influence has had such a profound effect on his own

Mallard drake by Don Briddell

Mallard drake by Don Briddell

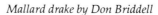

artistic direction.

As the Ward brothers grew older, their name became legendary. Their work had been featured in the *National Geographic Magazine.* In 1974 the Salisbury State College conferred upon them Honorary Doctor of Letters degrees. In 1980 the State of Maryland honoured them on a duck stamp by artist Jack Schroeder. They received the National Heritage Award from the National Endowment of the Arts in Washington DC. Lem Ward received a personal citation from the President of the United States.

Yet it was the high regard – the love even – in which they were held by fellow decoy artists whom they had inspired, that was perhaps their most touching testimony. They were unpretentious men who attributed little to themselves – in fact, they often referred to themselves as 'dumb old country

Pair of American Wigeon 'slicks' by Don Briddell

RIGHT: *These flying terns by Larry Barth, of Pennsylvania,
won for him the supreme prize at the 1986 World
Wildfowl Carving Championship at Ocean City.
They are now on permanent display at the
North American Wildfowl Art Museum.*

*This duck stamp, by Jack Schroeder, depicting a Ward
Brothers Pintail decoy was issued in 1981 by the Maryland
Department of Natural Resources, in honour of
the Ward Brothers*

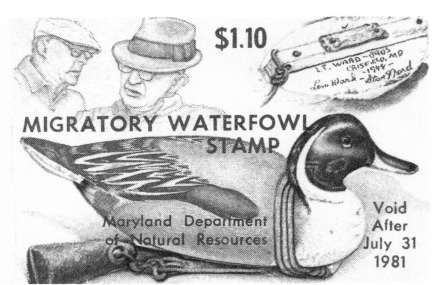

boys' – yet their work and example has touched the lives of thousands who have followed them in the art which they pioneered.

Steve died in 1976, aged 80. Following his paralysing stroke, Lem was never able to carve again, although he did manage to paint pictures until his death in 1984, at the age of 88.

L.T. Ward & Brother, Wildfowl Counterfeiters in Wood, carved an estimated 25,000 decoys during their long career. They inspired a new art movement and left behind a rich legacy of decoy art for collectors to cherish.

In 1968 a group of Eastern Shore businessmen and decoy enthusiasts, wishing to honour the Ward brothers and foster the growing decoy art movement they had inspired, founded the Ward Foundation. The Foundation has played a leading role in promot-

ing the art form and now has a large membership across America and, increasingly, overseas. Its main thrust has been to promote competitions and exhibitions. Every year since 1970 it has organised the highly successful World Championship Wildfowl Carving Competition held in the spring at the large Convention Center at Ocean City, Maryland.

A visit to 'the World' reveals something of the impact and magnitude of the decoy art movement. Here the visitor can see work of breathtaking quality and beauty, by professional carvers, side by side with the work of novices and amateurs. The thousands of exhibits create a wonderfully colourful and spectacular display. The judging of the many classes in the competition raises the level of excitement among competitors and spectators alike, with everyone trying to anticipate the judges' verdict. The

*The head carving competition attracts many fine entries.
1986 World Wildfowl Carving Competition*

judges have a difficult – some would say almost impossible – task selecting the winners, particularly when they reach the top professional classes. Most of the judging is done around a tank of water in which the birds must float at exactly the right trim and with total stability. This not only applies to the Shooting Stool (working decoy) classes but also to the highly decorative pieces. This maintains the strong link with the decoy origins of the art form.

Inevitably judging sometimes raises problems and as in any field of competition there is always discussion and some strongly held points of view on the subject. In 1987 the Ward Foundation took the initiative in bringing together experienced competition organisers and judges to thrash out a code of practice to bring judging into a more structured, standard framework, which can only be a good thing for the movement as a whole. Competition is clearly

*The theme for the 1986 World Wildfowl Carving
Championship was 'seabirds'. Carvers responded with a
wonderful display, including these superb Laughing Gulls.*

*Miniature carvings have great appeal and competition in
this class is as keen as in the life-size categories. 1986 World
Wildfowl Carving Competition*

moving towards an international dimension as interest spreads abroad. Already several small but successful competitions have been held in Britain.

A lasting impression of 'the World' is the atmosphere. The large crowds that pack the Ocean City Convention Center for the three days of the event are the most sociable and good-humoured imaginable. If you are interested in decoys, you are among some of the friendliest people I have ever come across.

To win at 'the World' is the pinnacle of accomplishment for any ambitious wildfowl carver and competition is intense. Each year the carving judged Best in Show is automatically purchased by the Ward Foundation for $20,000 and it then enjoys a permanent place of honour in the fine museum established by the Foundation at the Salisbury State College, Salisbury, Maryland.

The North American Wildfowl Art Museum

contains a fine range of decoy exhibits tracing the history of the decoy in North America. A collection of Ward brothers decoys and a mock-up of their workshop has pride of place and decoys representative of the various distinct regions are displayed for comparison. The winning pieces from the annual competition afford the visitor an opportunity to see how the standard of work has improved year by year – ample justification of the good work performed by the Ward Foundation. In 1987 the Ward Foundation mounted a special exhibition of wildfowl carvings at the internationally famous Smithsonian Museum in Washington. Each year in the fall, an exhibition is held in Salisbury which has proved a successful event for both artists and collectors.

LEFT: *The North American Wildfowl Art Musuem is housed in the Salisbury State College, Salisbury, Maryland*

BELOW: *Blue winged teal drake by John Garton of Smith's Falls, Ontario, winner of the World Championship in 1971. This fine decoy marked the end of the untextured era of competition decorative decoys. Subsequent winners used the feather texturing technique pioneered by the Reverend Jack Drake. North American Wildfowl Art Museum*

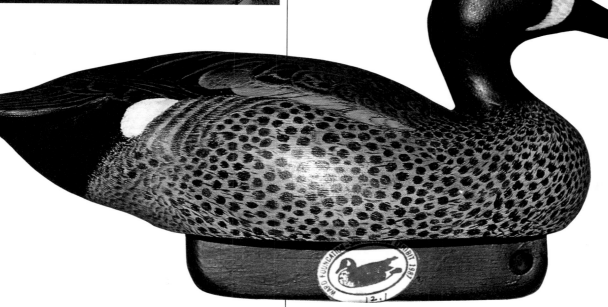

ABOVE: *Blue winged teal hen by John Garton. North American Art Museum*

RIGHT: *'Nuptial Aggression'. This pair of wigeon by Pat Godin, of Ontario, won Best in World in the Competition Grade Floating Pairs class at the World Championship in 1974. North American Wildfowl Art Musuem*

ABOVE AND BELOW: *Detail of 'Black-crowned Night Heron'*

RIGHT: *Best in World Decorative Life-size 'Black-crowned Night Heron' by Anthony J. Rudisill, of New Jersey. North American Wildfowl Art Museum*

THE DRIFTER

I'm just an old has-been decoy.
No ribbons I have won.
My sides and head are full of shot,
From many a blazing gun.
My home has been by the river,
Just drifting along with the tide.
No roof have I had for a shelter,
No place where I could abide.
I've rocked to winter's wild fury,
I've scorched in the heat of the sun.
I've drifted and drifted and drifted,
For tides never cease to run.
I was picked up by some fool collector,
Who put me up here on a shelf.
But my place is out on the river,
Where I can drift all by myself.
I want to go back to the shoreline,
Where flying clouds hang thick and low,
And get the touch of the rain drops,
And the velvety soft touch of the snow.

Steve Ward, 1971
(His last complete poem)

THE EASTON WATERFOWL
FESTIVAL

*The flying Swans in the hotel lobby of the Tidewater Inn
during the 1987 Festival are by Robert Kerr of Ontario,
Canada*

Another major event in the decoy art calèndar is the Easton Waterfowl Festival, held each year during November. Easton is a delightful small town some 50 miles north of Salisbury and situated close to the Chesapeake. It is a prosperous town with a heritage of fine colonial buildings, tree-lined avenues and a relaxed, friendly atmosphere. At a latitude of 38°45′N, the fall lingers late on the Eastern Shore and although the Festival is held during November, it usually seems to enjoy fine, sunny weather, which shows the town off at its best. In the run-up to Thanksgiving there are ripe orange pumpkins on the verandahs and vine wreaths on the doors of the houses. During the Festival the whole town gives itself over to celebrating the beauty and bounty of the waterfowl that every year return to winter on the Eastern Shore. To stand looking up at long skeins of honking Canada geese and beautiful white swans wheeling in the sky above Easton at sunset, is to

The elegant Tidewater Inn serves as General
Headquarters during the Easton Waterfowl Festival

ABOVE RIGHT: *Superb Gadwall drake exhibited at the Easton Waterfowl Festival*

BELOW RIGHT: *Pair of Pontail hens exhibited at the Easton Waterfowl Festival*

Standing in line to visit some of the very popular exhibitions at the Easton Waterfowl Festival

understand why the people of Easton hold their Waterfowl Festival.

The festival was held for the first time in 1971 and has grown steadily in attendance and popularity ever since. The civic buildings, schools, even the fire station are taken over and exhibitions and demonstrations of decoy and wildfowl art are held all over town. The fine Tidewater Hotel in the centre of the town becomes general headquarters for the organisers – all volunteers – who run the whole event with quite remarkable smoothness and efficiency. Since it started, over $1,000,000 has been raised to benefit waterfowl conservation and education.

Two bus lines, the blue and the orange, run a free and continuous service around town between the various venues. There is ample provision for good eating and refreshments. The event lasts for three days and there is so much to see that it is necessary to work quite hard to get around to all the exhibits within that time.

Thousands of fine decoys can be seen in the Easton High School buildings where dealers, collectors and carvers meet to buy, sell and swop decoys. On the

*Attractively displayed decoys at the Easton
Waterfowl Festival*

*Classic Redhead drake decoy by A. Elmer Cromwell.
Exhibited at the Easton Waterfowl Festival*

*One of my favourite decoys. Classic Mallard drake by
Illinois maker Charles Walker*

RIGHT: *All the top carvers exhibit at the Easton Waterfowl Festival. Ernest Muehlmatt, from Pennsylvania, is a distinguished carver who is noted for his superb rendition of small birds such as quail and woodcock*

Quail by Ernest Muehlmatt

*Magnificent Pintail drake by Illnois carver, John Gewerth.
John is in the top league of decorative decoy carvers and is a
consistent winner of awards at competitions. Easton
Waterfowl Festival*

day before the Festival opens, a major auction is held. In the old Armoury building you may see the fine decorative pieces of champion carvers who are there to discuss their work with you. Elsewhere the dealers in carving tools, materials and books do a brisk business with the many carvers who attend. During the Festival the World Championship Goose Calling Contest and the Mason Dixon Regional Duck Calling Contest are held; this always packs the large auditorium of the Easton High School to capacity. You may also visit several exhibitions of fine paintings by many of America's top wildfowl artists. For anyone interested in decoys, decoy carving, waterfowl and waterfowl art, the Easton Waterfowl Festival is sure to delight. The remarkable growth in its popularity is but another indication of the broad appeal that decoy art in particular and waterfowl art in general has for a great many people.

This attractive stand at the Easton Waterfowl Festival
exhibits the work of 'Hurricane Pete' Peterson

CHINCOTEAGUE

For the decoy enthusiast, no visit to the Eastern Shore would be complete without a visit to the island of Chincoteague.

Chincoteague is situated a mile or so off the coast of Virginia, to which it is connected by a causeway, one of the so-called 'barrier islands' separating the mainland from the perpetual onslaught of the Atlantic. From time to time dark storms and great pounding seas have swept the islands, bringing hardship to the small communities who make a sparse living from hunting and fishing.

Yet Chincoteague is normally a place of quiet beauty, its low-lying marshes, creeks and fragrant pine woods abounding with wildlife. Beyond Chincoteague the island of Assateague is now a National Wildlife Refuge where you can see many species of duck, geese and birds, including egrets, great blue heron and different kinds of shore birds. In the woods are white-tailed deer, sika deer and many small animals.

Not surprisingly, Chincoteague has produced a number of noteworthy decoy makers, the best known being Ira Hudson, Dave 'Umbrella' Watson (so-called because he always carried an umbrella in case it should rain), Miles Hancock and Doug Jester.

Before tourism and the Refuge brought the visitors who now account for much of the community's

Roe 'Ducman' Terry in his workshop. Roe is a hunting guide who makes excellent working decoys and decoy style decorative that are in great demand by collectors

BELOW: *This superb Brent goose decoy by Roe 'Ducman' Terry is everything that a good working decoy should be. The body is made of cork. By courtesy of the Decoy Gallery, Chewton Mendip, near Bath, Somerset*

Reggie Birch is a talented Chincoteague decoy carver, seen here in his workshop carving a full-size heron

BELOW: *Red breasted Merganser decoy by Reggie Birch of Chincoteague. Note fish held in bill!*
By courtesy of The Decoy Gallery, Chewton Mendip, near Bath, Somerset

Note that he uses a hand
axe for roughing out the
basic shape finishing up
with a spokeshave

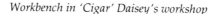

Workbench in 'Cigar' Daisey's workshop

income, most families made their living by fishing and waterfowl hunting. the result was a hardy breed of characters who were self-reliant, valued their freedom and adopted a somewhat insular attitude to outsiders. Yet mention of decoys brings a warmth of hospitality that soon makes you feel at home here.

On Chincoteague decoy-making was for real, part of hunting, part of a way of life which often involved sitting around a stove on cold winter evenings, carving and story-telling.

Arguably the best-known decoy carver in the world is one of the great characters and story-tellers of Chincoteague, Delbert 'Cigar' Daisey. An article on Chincoteague in a *National Geographic Magazine* article in 1980 carried a piece about Cigar, picturing

him in his workshop, together with a photograph of a beautiful prize-winning hen Pintail. Cigar tells how he received letters from over 50 countries following that *National Geographic* article, from people captivated by the Pintail and wishing to know more about his art.

Since those days, countless visitors to America have made their way specially to Chincoteague to visit this apparently rather reserved and shy man. He is at his best sharing a beer or two with friends in his workshop. Then he opens up and in no time at all is in great form. His life on the marshes where he hunted and fished to make a living, provides a wonderful fund of tales which can keep his listeners enthralled. Sometimes in his early days his method of illegally trapping ducks put him somewhat on the

'Cigar Daisey's workshop is at the water's edge looking out
across the marshes towards Assateague

The famous 'Cigar' Daisey brand appears on the bottom of his decoys and on his anchor weights

wrong side of the law. It was while emptying such a trap, that he dropped a King Edward cigar, which was just the evidence that the local game warden needed to detect the culprit. He has been known as 'Cigar' ever since and this brand is marked on the base of all his decoys and on his decoy weights. His days as an outlaw hunter are long since past. As he points out, it meant keeping very unsocial hours and it was 'a right cold' job. Now he prefers to keep warm and comfortable in his workshop.

Cigar Daisey's workshop is without doubt the most delightful I have ever visited. It is beautifully situated, looking out over the marshes towards Assateague lighthouse. There is a small dock outside

This huge swan decoy made and used by 'Cigar' Daisey was so conspicuous that it sometimes gave away his whereabouts to the local Game Warden. It was 'retired' from active service and now occupies a place of honour, most decoratively, in the Refuge Waterfowl Museum

 *BELOW: Bufflehead decoys by 'Cigar' Daisey*

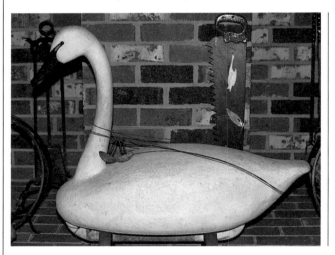

where he keeps his boats. As you look out over the marshes a great blue heron flaps lazily by. He has so many visitors I wondered how he ever managed to do any work. Cigar was philosophical. 'It used to be hard to make a living,' he said. 'Now people pay me good money for a decoy and I've more work than I can handle. I'm grateful for that.'

Cigar's workshop is highly mechanised. In addition to his bandsaw he has no less than five flexible shaft power carving tools by his bench – 'to save time fooling around changing bits all day' – and he has the latest Japanese reciprocating chisel.

Cigar Daisey carves a wide range of subjects – swans, geese, duck, confidence decoys and shore birds, both working and decorative. His work reflects a lifetime of close familiarity with the birds he carves. Everything he makes has great appeal and is

This fabulous display of yellowleg shorebird decoys by 'Cigar' Daisey, demonstrates his artistic and creative versatility. Refuge Waterfowl Museum

Rare Canada goose decoy by Lem and Lee Dudley of Knotts Island, Virginia. Refuge Waterfowl Museum, Chincoteague

highly collectable. His carving career has spanned the years of development of decoy art, indeed he has contributed greatly to its development.

Cigar is 'resident carver' at the Refuge Waterfowl Museum in Chincoteague, founded by John Maddox, a local businessman. Although Cigar is seldom there, fine examples of his work can be seen. Whole rigs of decoys hang on pegs and there are hundreds, probably thousands, of fine decoys on display, many of them old and valuable, many by contemporary carvers.

The museum is a great tribute to the island's carvers and to its founder John Maddox, who had the vision and good judgment to recognise the beauty and importance of these decoys and to preserve them for public display in such a setting. Here you can see decoys as they should be seen, in a way that brings real meaning to the term 'decoy art'. It is a delightful place and should not be missed if you can possibly get there.

The big decoy event of the year on Chincoteague is the Easter Decoy Festival which attracts decoy enthusiasts from far and wide. The 1987 Festival was especially memorable for me as I had the great good

*This realistic replica of a decoy carver's workshop is to be
seen at the Refuge Waterfowl Museum, Chincoteague*

LEFT: *'The Dollar Duck'. In the days of market hunting, the little Ruddy duck was known as the 'dollar duck' — that being the price it made at market. By comparison the Canvasback made four dollars. This Ruddy duck decoy, made by 'Cigar' Daisey, was won by the author in the raffle at the Chincoteague Easter Decoy Festival. The price of the ticket? One dollar!*

RIGHT: *Heron by Tad Beach*

Chincoteague Easter Festival posters. Designed by local artist Hal Lott, these posters have become very collectable

Eastern Shore carver Tad Beach

fortune to win the big prize in the raffle — a much coveted Ruddy Duck drake carved and presented by Cigar Daisey!

To the south of Chincoteague lies Cobb Island, once the home of Nathan Cobb, one of the most acclaimed decoy makers of all time. Eastern Shore carver Tad Beach grew up on his grandfather's farm which looked out over the water to Cobb Island. His grandfather had over 100 decoys and young Tad grew up in a world where hunting and decoys were part of everyday life. He developed an early interest in birds, being especially fascinated by hawks and

herons. He started to carve 20 years ago when he was only nine years old. He has been entering exhibitions with his work since 1968 so his carving career has spanned the great development period of decorative decoy carving. He remembers visiting the Ward brothers and being greatly inspired by their work. He says he has also been influenced by the work of a number of carvers seen at shows and competitions but was especially inspired by the work of Grainger McCoy, one of the great artists in this field.

He enjoys making miniatures, which he finds have a strong appeal to collectors but his favourite subject

LEFT: *Red Tailed Hawk carved by Eastern Shore carver, Tad Beach. In the collection of Dr and Mrs Cornelius Frey, Maryland*

BELOW: *Head detail of Red Tailed Hawk by Tad Beach*

is hawks. He makes two or three of these magnificent full-sized birds in a year, spending hundreds of hours working to achieve the finest possible detail in both the carving and the painting. The result is a stunning work of art which places this quiet unassuming young man high among the ranks of the best in American decorative bird carving.

There are a number of carvers who have rejected the realistic style of decorative decoy carving with its inserts and feather detail. Instead they have chosen to follow decoy making in the traditional form. Their work is nevertheless decorative in that very rarely – if ever – would a collector be tempted to hunt over their decoys. Yet such work evokes all the nostalgia of the finest old working decoys; the strong simple form, the pleasing tactility of the wood and the mellowness of the paint patina.

Without doubt, the most exciting carver in this

Mark McNair

school is Mark McNair. McNair moved to the Eastern Shore from New England some years ago and now lives in a remote but idyllic waterside home on the shore of the Chesapeake. Unlike most Eastern Shore carvers, McNair did not grow up with decoys. He was introduced to decoy carving by a friend in New England when he was in his twenties. He drew inspiration from the work of the great decoy makers of the past and carves in a style that reflects a deep respect for their methods of carving and painting.

Apart from his bandsaw (which was commonly used by many of the great master decoy makers) he uses no machine tools, preferring to use hand tools only. He will spend as long as it takes to complete a carving — for McNair the challenge of perfection is all that matters. His carvings have a style and stamp

RIGHT: *This exquisite carving of a dove in Mark McNair's workshop shows the simple grace of his work*

BELOW LEFT: *Red Breasted Merganser decoy by Mark McNair. This fine decoy has an 'inletted' head, that is, a finely worked dovetail arrangement enabling the head to be removed*

BELOW: *Mark McNair with a shorebird which has an inletted (dovetailed) head*

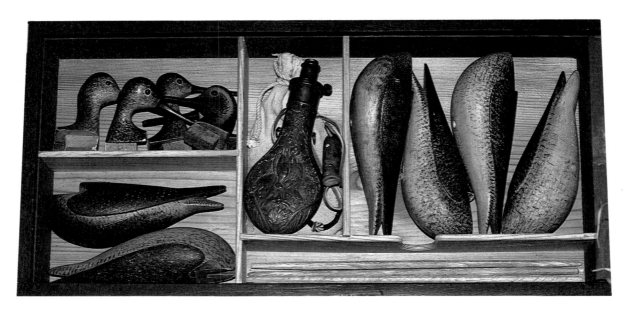

Small rig of yellowleg shorebird decoys in their own carrying case. Very much a novelty item but this superb piece of work had collectors fascinated at the Easton Waterfowl Festival

BELOW: *Mallard drake decoy by Mark McNair*

which is uniquely his own; the manner of their making is often quite remarkable. His shore birds may be hollow and have dovetailed, inletted heads. He will sometimes join two halves of a hollow duck by pegging the pieces of wood together to avoid using glue. His decoys are painted in a manner that suggests they have been around for 50 years during which time they have been lovingly handled by appreciative hands.

McNair's work can hold its own with that of any of the great carvers of the past. It is being keenly collected by the cognoscenti of the decoy collecting world and must be a joy to own.

William Gibian is another Eastern Shore carver who produces fine decoy style decorative carvings in the traditional way, eschewing mechanical tools and feather burners in favour of draw knives, spokeshaves and hand chisels.

Of Armenian stock – 'Just say I'm an old rug trader' – Gibian had no connection with decoys

William Gibian with pair of Dowitcher shorebirds

BELOW: *William Gibian working on a Curlew. He uses only handtools, apart from his bandsaw*

Superb preening yellowleg decoy by William Gibian. By
courtesy of The Decoy Gallery, Chewton Mendip, near
Bath, Somerset

Yellowleg shorebird decoy by William Gibian. The fine
carving and painting achieved by Gibian gives his
birds a classic quality that appeals strongly to
discerning collectors. By courtesy of The Decoy
Gallery, Chewton Mendip, near Bath, Somerset

*Cinnamon teal by William Gibian. By courtesy of
The Decoy Gallery, Chewton Mendip, near
Bath, Somerset*

until 1980 when a cousin's husband, a carver, challenged him to carve a bird. He made a shore bird from walnut and while it might not have won any prizes, it certainly proved to Gibian that he had aptitude and that he enjoyed carving. He had always had a fascination for three-dimensional form and the flowing curves of well designed motor cars, his favourite being the 'D' type Jaguar sports car. He had cherished the idea of being an automobile designer but, as so often happens in life, ended up as a construction worker.

He had a very artistic mother, so had grown up with drawing and paints and no doubt this helped him when it came to designing and painting his own early carvings. He read books on decoys and grew particularly attracted to shore birds. It is these that he has become best known for, although he does superb ducks as well.

After he had been carving for some time, he took some work to a decoy show at Virginia Beach and

Cockerel by William Gibian

had so many orders that it was not long before he was able to carve full time for a living.

He has a delightful studio close to his home, not far from the Atlantic shore where he can study the shore birds whose likenesses he captures so perfectly in wood.

Occasionally, Bill Gibian takes time off to carve a special piece as a birthday or Christmas present for his wife Carol. Can you imagine her pleasure on being presented with such marvellous works of art as the cat and the cockerel?

This delightful cat carved by William Gibian for his wife Carol, shows the versatility of both his carving and his painting

*Pair of Redhead decoys by Robert Litzenberg in the classic
Havre de Grace style*

View across the famous Susquehanna Flats from the new Havre de Grace Decoy Museum

Havre de Grace is a small town on the western shore of the mouth of the Susquehanna River, which flows south into the northern end of the Chesapeake Bay.

Just off the shore are the Susquehanna Flats which were, in their time, the scene of waterfowl hunting on a truly grand scale. The reason for this was the vast number of waterfowl that gathered there to feed on wild celery that grew in the soft mud of the bay. This in turn imparted to the ducks, mainly Canvasbacks, a superb flavour which made them succulent eating and hence very much in demand.

In the early years of this century the town thrived on the business generated by market hunting and the many sporting hunters who came to shoot here. Havre de Grace decoy makers turned out large numbers of sturdy decoys which over the years had developed a distinct Havre de Grace style. Each year without fail the wildfowl came, migrating south with the onset of winter. Each year the hunters took their toll, seeming to have no effect on the great flocks of

Decoy art at its most natural pictured here in a street of
Havre de Grace

R. Madison Mitchell, one of the grand old men of decoy making, pictured here at the Havre de Grace Decoy Museum with a Canvasback drake decoy made in his younger days

I have heard the same from another famous Havre de Grace decoy maker, Madison Mitchell, also now in his eighties, who still lives in the town.

Then in the 1930s disaster struck. Madison Mitchell takes up the story.

> A great hurricane from the south east whipped up the waters of the bay and tore the celery out of the flats and piled it high along the shore. As soon as we saw this we knew we had a disaster on our hands. Without the wild celery the birds would have no food. We contacted the authorities and tried to get help to replant the celery. It would have been easy to collect it and drop it back into the bay, where it would have rerooted itself. But time was against us and the authorities didn't respond with help. The wild celery was lost and that was the end of everything.

At about this time, another situation was developing which was to prove disastrous to waterfowl. The great wetlands in Canada, where the birds went to raise their young, were being drained to create more land for agriculture. In no time at all those great, wonderful flocks of ducks, geese and swans were down to a mere handful. The situation has never recovered. The Susquehanna River itself has been dammed for hydro electricity in several places, which has also altered the natural state of things and industry up river has added pollution to the problem.

I asked whether the efforts of organisations such as Ducks Unlimited had helped to improve matters by restoring some of the Canadian wetlands. Could not new celery beds be planted? As we looked out over the flats together, Mitchell shook his head sadly. 'The bottom used to be soft mud which was just right for the celery. Now all the stuff coming down the river has formed a hard crust over the mud and the celery won't grow any more.'

Out of this sad story one good thing remains, the legacy of wooden birds made by Havre de Grace decoy makers. Recently a fine new museum has been opened to honour their work and exhibit it for posterity. Madison Mitchell makes his way down to the museum most Sunday afternoons and his pride

birds that flew in. In 1982 I had the great pleasure of spending an afternoon hearing about those days from Paul Gibson, one of the old-time Havre de Grace decoy makers, in his workshop. Already well into his eighties, he nevertheless remembered clearly the excitement of the days when the ducks, geese and swans came in such numbers that they 'cut off the light from the sun'. Paul Gibson died in 1985 but

ABOVE: *The Havre de Grace Decoy Musuem*

Mock-up of Madison Mitchell's workshop showing him, as ever, smartly dressed in the bow-tie he wore every day of his working life

is evident as he meets a new generation of decoy enthusiasts who come to enjoy his work and talk to the old man. He will sign decoys which people bring in to show him and shakes his head in wonder at the prices people have paid – often thousands of dollars – to aquire a decoy he sold for no more than a few dollars years ago.

There is a realistic wax 'dummy' – his word, not mine, I would have chosen 'effigy' – showing Mitchell chopping out decoys , dressed as he was every day of his working life in a smart bow tie. Mitchell combined the work of mortician with his decoy making, so had to keep himself suitably dressed. There is also a very cleverly contrived scene constructed from a 1942 photograph of Madison, Paul Gibson, Robert McGaw and Lou Klair sitting around the stove in Mitchell's workshop.

The museum contains a large pool where in due course there will be a floating sink box surrounded by decoys depicting the typical Susquehanna flats method of hunting, prior to 1934 when the sink box was banned.

The museum is very well worth a visit and I hope that Madison Mitchell – one of the grand old men of decoy making – will be there for many more years to greet you.

This preeening Woodduck drake by Madison Mitchell is the
sort of decoy that every collector would love to own. Havre
de Grace Decoy Museum Collection.

RIGHT: Head of a swan decoy by Madison Mitchell

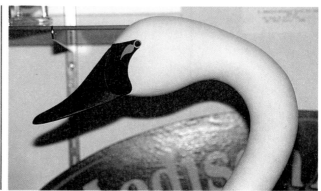

Pair of sturdy Canvasback decoys by Robert Litzenberg.
Note the anchor weights and lines

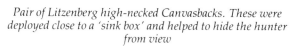

Decoy maker Robert Litzenberg outside his workshop

Pair of Litzenberg high-necked Canvasbacks. These were deployed close to a 'sink box' and helped to hide the hunter from view

Unusual hanging ducks in the collection of
Robert Litzenberg

*This old, rare Pintail by John Blair is a classic Delaware
River decoy in the collection of Robert Litzenberg*

Not far from Havre de Grace lives another old-timer whose work is also displayed in the Museum. He is Robert Litzenberg, now 77 years old and still chopping out decoys in his workshop as he has done since the 1930s. He also hunted a great deal, not as a market hunter but more as a guide for sporting hunters. He reels off many famous names who have been his hunting friends down the years and whose decoy collections have Litzenberg birds among them. His decoys have a lower tail than the typical Havre de Grace design. As he correctly observes, 'Most diving ducks carry their tails on the water, not above it.'

He has a fine collection of decoys by many other makers. This is a trait one often observes with carvers – they are also keen collectors. Many of these would be acquired by trading decoy for decoy but not always. I was amused when he told me how he had

Work in progress: part of the production line in Robert Litzenberg's workshop

agreed to sell someone a decoy by Henry Lockard in 1975 for $160, only to buy it back, having thought better of it, for $800 in 1987.

Robert Litzenberg decoys continue to sell better then ever before and, asked about delivery time, he seriously doubts being around long enough to complete his orders! Most of Robert Litzenberg's decoys are made of pine and his workshop is a model of orderly production method. Long may he enjoy making 'floating sculpture' for future generations to cherish.

The Susquehanna River carves its way through high ground in Pennsylvania to reach the Chesapeake Bay and the sea. Above the Holtwood dam, the land rises steeply and from a place known as The Pinnacle there is a fine commanding view of the great river hundreds of feet below. Close by, in an attractive area surrounded by woods, lives a talented decoy carver whose work is in an attractive style, both decorative and traditional. Bill Porterfield makes a wide variety of birds, mostly chopped from old telegraph poles or barn beams. He likes to give to his carvings a feeling

In addition to being a decoy maker, Robert Litzenberg also makes fine furniture. His workshop is a model of orderly method. He is seen here at his chopping block chopping out decoy bodies with a razor sharp axe

Bill Porterfield at work on a Canada Goose decoy

BELOW: *Red-breasted Merganser decoy by Bill Porterfield. The crest at the back of the head is of horsehair*

of age and 'woodiness', emphasising the grain and character of the wood. He is a very engaging character with a keen sense of humour; a visit to his workshop is always fun. Bill's wife Pat is an artistic homemaker in the traditional American country style and it is no wonder that visitors are inspired to go away with a Porterfield decoy to add charm to their own home.

Part of the Porterfield home is self-contained guest accommodation. Guests may stay for a week or more to enjoy the many attractions of this delightful area of Pennsylvania and spend time learning how to carve in Bill's workshop.

Decorative heron carving by Bill Porterfield

RIGHT: *Pair of Litzenberg decoys from the collection of Bill and Pat Porterfield*

BELOW: *'Stick-up' decoys were commonly used in cornfields after harvesting to lure in Canada geese. The hunters would conceal themselves in a 'goose pit' nearby*

Bob White pictured in his workshop on the banks of the Delaware River

BELOW: *Bob White's workshop. Work in progress*

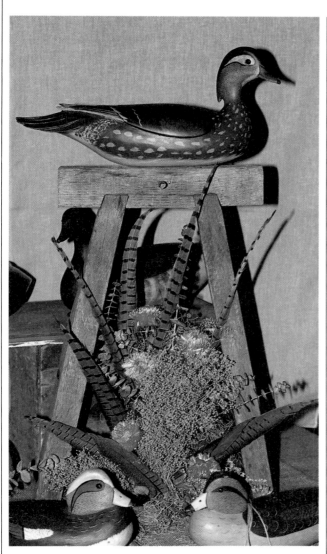

Pauline White is very skilled at displaying her husband's superb decoys when they attend shows together, as this picture shows

DELAWARE RIVER

The Delaware River was another broad waterway that attracted large numbers of waterfowl. They in turn attracted hunters who used fine decoys and their own special techniques to stalk their quarry. Decoy maker and hunter Bob White explained how, as he showed me a fine Delaware River scull boat in his boathouse by the river above Philadelphia. It was made in the thirties and its wooden frames and planks are as good today as then, thanks to the care it receives from its owner. It is a low freeboard boat of about 15 feet in length, with a short foredeck around which camouflage was arranged to conceal the hunter. A curved sculling oar passed through the stern enabling the hunter to lie low in the boat while gently propelling it along by sculling with the oar.

'The plan was to set out the rig (of decoys) in a suitable spot, then wait uptide until the ducks came into the decoys. You then sculled gently down tide toward the ducks until you were close enough to get a good shot at them.' This called for stealth, good boatmanship and decoys that not only pulled the birds in but were convincing enough to hold them there until you could get down to them. The best-known decoy makers in this region were John English and John Blair, and their decoys are among the most attractive you will find. Bob White came into hunting just at the end of the great hunting era on the Delaware, before the waterfowl became scarce. He counts himself lucky to have seen those days and now keeps the Delaware tradition of decoy making alive by carving fine decoys constructed of the same material — white cedar — and hollowed in the way that was traditionally used in this area. The smell of cedar wood in a decoy workshop is pure delight, as were the decoys I saw on the work bench, when I visited Bob and his wife Pauline. They have a fine old house in which Pauline expresses her own creativity, complementing Bob's decoys with beautiful flower arrangements and her collection of hand-made baskets. Decoys are an integral part of traditional American country decor and it is a joy to see them alongside quilts, painted furniture, floral wreaths and basketry — they somehow all blend together into a richly textural and colourful visual feast. Pauline travels with her husband to decoy

Another fine example of how decoys can be displayed decoratively. Decor by Pauline White. Decoys by her husband, Bob White

RIGHT: Elegant Merganser decoy by Bob White

This little Snipe decoy, from Bob and Pauline White's collection, certainly makes the most elegant decorative object, although I fear that with such a slender neck it would have had to be used with great care by the hunter

shows and their stand always has an extra special appeal, thanks to her artistry.

I asked Bob if his decoys were ever actually used these days. He said that some people used them a few times just to give them a taste of the water, then they were taken home to be enjoyed as decorative art. He and his wife have a fine collection of Delaware decoys and several others that they cherish. One is a Ward decoy that Bob found washed up on the shore. 'It had seen better days: all the paint was gone but basically it was a good decoy,' Bob told me. 'I took it home and next time we went down the Eastern Shore I went to Crisfield and asked Lem if he could do a repaint for me. He said he would and sometime later we had a letter saying the decoy was ready for collection and we had better bring plenty of money with us! When we picked it up, there was, of course, no charge. Lem had had his little joke, and on the bottom he made this inscription.'

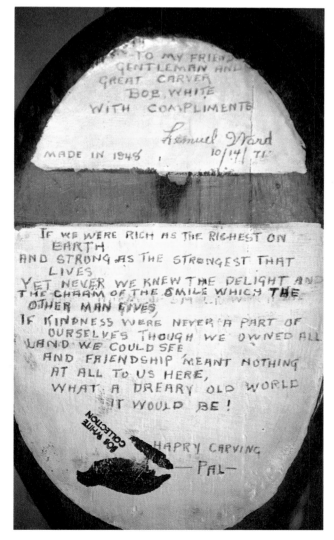

LOUISIANA

*This delightful little Louisiana teal decoy is the sort of gem
every collector dreams of*

Classic Louisiana Pintail drake by Nicol Vidacovitch.
Collection of Curt Fabre

The great Mississippi River is a major flyway for the millions of birds that migrate from the northern summer breeding grounds in Canada to the milder climate of the south where they winter.

Every fall, the lakes, swamps and bayous of Louisiana are the destination of vast numbers of migrating waterfowl, notably scaup, pintail and blue-winged teal. Here they have always provided plentiful hunting and it is therefore no surprise to find that decoys have been used for as long as can be remembered by the hunters of this region. Yet their emergence as part of decoy history has been revealed only in recent years, largely due to the dedicated and painstaking research of Charles W. Frank Jnr., author of *Wetland Heritage – The Louisiana Duck Decoy*. In the first and now classic work on American decoys, *Wild Fowl Decoys* published in 1934 by Joel Barber, he wrote:

> That great region lying south of the Carolinas and west along the Gulf of Mexico, has never gone in for native decoy making. Although using decoys to a considerable extent, the southern gunners relied on the northern factories to supply them, principally those of the Middle West. In recent years the south has developed its own factories but the situation remains unchanged for there are practically no hand makers. Surprising but true.
>
> On the other hand, I have always looked forward to finding decoys made by Seminole Indians or decoys of hewn cypress by denizens of the Bayous along the Gulf States or the great marshes on the delta of the Mississippi. But no. So far, only factory stools (mass produced decoys) and in recent years live decoys gradually displacing artificial lures.
>
> There is, however, one exception: the Canada Geese 'profiles' used by gunners on the sand bars of the Mississippi River. These decoys are made locally and have been for many years. They are similar in every way to the 'profiles' employed in the cut-over wheat fields of western states, made of wood, sheet iron or tin. The 'stick-up' idea, of course, is very ancient; first employed by aborigines in killing waterfowl on land. The manner of adoption on southern

Mallard drake decoy by Mark Whipple. Collection of Curt Fabre

gunning grounds cannot be definitely arrived at.

Intuitively, however, he doubted his findings, for he ends this chapter by saying:

It is too much to ask of a collector to believe that fowlers of the deep south missed the great American impulse to make decoy ducks.

Well, his hunch was right, as Charles Frank has so adequately proved. And for the romantic collector who regards decoys not just as the handsome objects they are, or as financial investments but also as an evocation of the life and times of the men who made and used them, what a rich area this proves to be!

The delta of the Mississippi River spreads out over thousands of square miles of flat land interspersed with vast areas of swamp and marsh linked by lakes and channels known locally as bayous. During its history the great river has carved out many different channels to the sea and only in fairly recent history has the river to some extent been controlled by the building of levees or banks which contain its flood waters.

Another factor which exercises a powerful influence over the area are the hurricanes which between the months of July to October are prone to come howling in from the Gulf of Mexico creating havoc, destroying homes and causing tidal waves and flooding far inland. Only those who have experienced hurricanes, either on land or sea, can truly realise the savagery of these storms. In recent memory the hurricane of 1969 caused widespread destruction along the gulf coast. Who can say how many fine old decoys were swept out of homes and boat sheds and lost forever?

Thanks to the work of those collectors and decoy historians who have recognised the importance of researching the history of decoy making in Louisiana, there are enough fine examples in safe

Louisiana maker Mitchel Lafrance made superb decoys such
as this beautiful Pintail drake

Classic Pintail decoy by Louisiana maker Clovis Vizier.
Collection of Tan Brunet

keeping now for future generations to enjoy. This is important, for perhaps nowhere is the link between folk art and fine art decoys stronger than in this Louisiana bayou country.

The people who settled the swamplands of the Mississippi delta area were the former French settlers from Newfoundland, the Acadians, who when displaced by the British, wandered across America surviving mainly as hunters and trappers until the Spanish, who at that time ruled Louisiana, recognising them as devout Catholics, gave them sanctuary, and the right to settle during the eighteenth century.

Here the place names and family names are mainly French and the people are known as Cajuns (Acadians). Whilst every bit American, they still retain a distinctive culture and to this day frequently resort to a French patois among themselves. They are lively, hard-working and delightfully hospitable people, quick to seize any excuse for a celebration or party ('Laissez les bon temps rouler!') and endowed with a sense of perseverance, which enables them to survive and rebuild after hurricanes. They have survived by fishing – fortunately the seas off the delta are teeming with fine shrimps and fish – and hunting the swamps for alligator, nutria pelts and wildfowl. In recent times the offshore oil industry in the Mexican Gulf has brought plenty of work and prosperity, although at the time of writing the oil industry is suffering something of a slump which is affecting the area.

The art of decorative decoy carving has today spread widely across America but I think it may be justly claimed that no one area has produced so many top class carvers as this. The Cajuns seem to possess an innate artistic ability which expresses itself in the things they know best, the beautiful wildfowl which are so much part of the heritage of this place. To visit these fellow carvers I travelled west and south from New Orleans to Bayou Lafourche, one of the major bayous of the delta which serves as high street to a number of small towns that lie along it.

It has already been suggested that in each of the distinct areas of decoy carving, it is usual to find a predominant carver whose decoys' style and design exercised an influence on other carvers in that area. The major influence along Bayou Lafourche appears to have come via the Vizier family.

Third generation Cajun decoy carver Captain Jimmy Vizier is acclaimed for both working and decorative decoys

Third generation decoy carver Captain Jimmy Vizier has been part of the bridge structure between the working decoy past and the fine art decoys of the present. His grandfather, Beauregard Vizier, lived from 1848 to 1933 and made his living by trapping and fishing. He is known to have carved decoys for his own use in hunting waterfowl to help feed his family of ten children. Of these, three sons, Clovis, Beauregard and Odee turned out to be talented decoy carvers. Odee taught his son Jimmy to carve, and found in him great aptitude. Jimmy's brother, 'Black' Vizier, is also a fine carver. Jimmy Vizier has turned out to be one of the greatest and best-known

Mallard drake decoys by Odee Vizier

*This superb shorebird carving by Jimmy Vizier shows the
wide range of his talent*

Cajun carvers, having won innumerable prizes at shows and competitions for both working decoys and fine decorative decoy carvings.

The Vizier influence touched another young Cajun, Andrew 'Tan' Brunet, who lived nearby and eagerly came to learn all he could of decoy carving from Odee and his son Jimmy, who is some five years older than Tan. Odee died in 1969 but Jimmy and Tan continued to develop their talents, turning out to be one of the most powerful forces in the development of decorative decoy art.

Jimmy is a tug boat operator in the offshore oil business and for him carving remains a recreational pursuit. He finds time in a busy schedule to carve for competitions and attends a number of the major shows. Tan went on to become five times World Champion.

There is a nice twist to round off this Vizier story. There is no son to carry on the decoy tradition of the family. But Jimmy Vizier is the proud father of three very beautiful daughters. At one of the decoy competitions, his youngest daughter Jessica met and fell

*Canada goose decorative decoy. Collection of Captain
Jimmy Vizier*

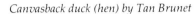

Canvasback duck (hen) by Tan Brunet

in love with a handsome young Canadian carver, World Champion Pat Godin. They married and now have a young son. With such a pedigree, who knows what the future may hold for him!

The name Tan Brunet is legendary to everyone in the world of decoy art. If there is a champion of champions among contemporary carvers, then Tan Brunet must surely be that man, having won the World Championship no less than five times in 1977, 1978, 1981, 1982 and 1983. Tan is a flamboyant character with a larger than life personality. He is a fine master of ceremonies at the annual New Orleans decoy show; he has been known to jump exuberantly into the judges' water tank at Ocean City on being announced winner at the World Championship. In his workshop I found an energetic and hard-working man; at home a man dedicated to his family, and a genuinely kind and hospitable host. What makes the Brunet legend even more remarkable is the emergence of his son Jett, now in his mid-twenties, as a champion carver in his own right. A younger son Jude works as a deckhand on a shrimp boat; during my visit he, too, was working on a fine picture of flying swans which he was entering for a duck stamp

ABOVE: *Detail of Canvasback*

LEFT: *Close up of the miniature Canvasback decoy — complete with tiny anchor weight — which adds such appeal to this superb carving by Tan Brunet*

ABOVE: *Miniature Pintail drake by Tan Brunet*

RIGHT: *Evening carving session at the Brunet workshop*

Scaup drake decoy by Jett Brunet. Although this carving is beautifully decorative, it is made as a working decoy. Note the robust thickness of the tail, designed to stand up to the rigours of hunting

competition. Tan and Jett share the same workshop and it is characteristic of the Cajun lifestyle and extreme sociability that most evenings friends drop by, and maybe four or five Cajuns will carve, swop stories, discuss decoy shows and generally enjoy light-hearted banter. World Champion carver he might be and greatly respected for it, but that did not stop his sons Jett, Jude and close friends Dan Danos and Rudi Guidry, groaning in mock horror when Tan produced some of his poetry for me at one evening session during my visit. They advise him to stay away from poetry and concentrate on his carving. Tan is an emotional man not ashamed to share tears of joy with his family when he or Jett wins another big prize at the World or the other competitions which they attend. Likewise if he feels moved to express emotional thoughts he does so through spontaneous poetry which, if not in the same league as Longfellow and Wordsworth, certainly tells us something of the warmth and sincerity of this likeable man. His tribute to Lem Ward is sincere and touching.

A TRIBUTE TO LEM WARD

Come ride the wind with me
Right next to the Lord.
And he'll point out his love work
In a man called Lem Ward.

Over the Chesapeake we soar
Next to the sand dunes
And unto the shore.

Crisfield's the town,
And the time is yesteryear.
I'll tell you of a legend
If you but lend me your ear.

The call is of the wild goose.
His da-coys are many,
And prized by the wise.
Even the derelicts
Are not cast aside.

His life reads like a fairy tale,
As if planned to the hilt.
Wildowl Art is the victor,
Cause Lem never quit.

Now the world is much richer
For having gazed on his soul.
He wants it that way
As he once wrote and told.

And the wind is sweet here.
The food is of the sea;
The clam boats at the pier.

This tale is of a man,
Or is he some sort of god.
No, he's just a genius
With the dreams of a child.

His mind has no hate,
His body no doom;
Cause the Lord filled it with peace
And for else there's no room.

'Song and rhyme
Love of Life
Peace with men
His lifelong strife.'

This poem of sorts,
With me at the helm;
Tells of my respect,
For this man they call Lem.

In his hands there's magic,
Cause his mark shows of care.
You can't help but wonder,
Did he get my share?

But share he will,
Or give it to you all.
If you but ask
He will beckon to your call.

His poems he has lent
With no charge for their gold.
Shakespeare's head would be bent
When Lem's story is told.

When the snow was adrift
And the watermen ashore;
He chopped at a da-coy,
Next to the pot belly stove.

Books have been written
And a legend is born;
Museums are built
As part of his throne.

Now the story is spent
And is long overdue.
All the ribbons we've won
Can be traced back to you.

Hey Lem, sip a little Maxwell
And light up a Pall.
The world needs another poem
And boy, can you do it well!

So here's to the King,
A bouquet from the heart,
This poem from all carvers
A tribute to Lem Ward.

The old decoy is a Louisiana classic by Clovis Vizier and is surely folk art at its very best. From the collection of Tan Brunet. The Mallard drake by Jett Brunet represents the leading edge of the art form which evolved from such beginnings

*Canvasback decoy by Jett Brunet during the carving stage.
Capturing, as it does, the very essence of the stately 'Can',
is it not a superb piece of sculpture as it stands?*

I hope that Tan does go on writing his poetry; it is from the heart, just as it was with the Ward brothers themselves, who loved life and friends and often said so in verse.

The Brunet method of carving is not typical. They use large pieces of tupelo, a superb carving wood from the swamps of Louisiana and take the whole duck in one piece, head included, straight out of the block, using just a hand saw and a razor-sharp hand axe.

The pattern is pencilled roughly on the wood as they work, but it is clear that they have the ability to see the whole three-dimensional composition of the bird with maybe turned head and raised wings as they rough it out. I am not even sure that 'rough out' is the correct term, for the work with the axe is so fine that on completion of this stage the form of the bird is well established. Then, using finely honed knives, the detailed carving is accomplished with sure, deft cuts. A simple and effective tool known as a 'scorp' is used to scoop out grooves in shaping the side pocket contours.

Head detail of Canvasback decoy by Jett Brunet

LEFT: *A piece of tupelo and a razor sharp carving axe. Tan Brunet at work chopping out a decoy*

RIGHT: *An unusual and useful tool known as a scorp, used by the Brunets during the shaping of the duck. The tool is said to be of ancient origin*

*Mallard drake by Jett Brunet. The remarkable skill and
artistry of this brilliant young Cajun artist is clearly
demonstrated in this superb carving*

Tail detail of Mallard drake by Jett Brunet. Note the separation of the tail feathers and the shape of the outside edge of the large tertial feather, where it rests on the lower primary feathers

The hallmark of Brunet carving is not only fine composition, giving a lifelike attitude to the duck but superb detail and texturing, so fine that you have to marvel at the patience and care that must go into achieving it. The final stage of painting is accomplished using oil paints, something which is common in Louisiana, less so in other areas where most carvers use acrylic paint. Asked why oils were used in preference to acrylics, the Brunets told me that softer tones and blending could be achieved with oil paints. At the painting stage, Jett confessed, they do go off somewhere quiet to work alone in order to be able to concentrate without any distractions. When you study the superb painting of their work you understand why. Both Tan and Jett, and indeed others in their close circle of Cajun carvers, produce work of stunning quality. Jimmy Vizier describes Tan as 'a natural'. At every stage of the complex processes of producing a World Championship quality carving, in the composition, the carving, the feather texturing, the painting and presentation, he brings to his work perfection and artistic genius. The

ABOVE: *Redhead drake by Jett Brunet*

LEFT: *Head detail of Redhead drake by Jett Brunet*

*This carving of a Mallard drake collected top honours in its
class at the 1986 World Championship*

same can be said of his son Jett.

Every year, accompanied by his charming wife Jan, son Jett and his wife Rhonda, and other wildfowl carvers from the bayous, Tan leads a Cajun raiding party to the World Championships at Ocean City. Tan is not keen on flying, so the convoy drives for three days from Louisiana to Maryland. I imagine it must be quite a party, especially on the way home when there is invariably plenty to celebrate, as the Cajuns' record for winning at competitions is formidable.

As might be expected, the Brunet order book is always full and both Tan and Jett work hard to keep up with their commissions. Even so, Tan has found time to paint five beautiful oil paintings of waterfowl to celebrate each of his World Championships. These are produced as limited edition signed prints and are greatly prized by decoy enthusiasts and collectors.

Green Winged Teal. Oil painting by Tan Brunet

*Head of Canvasback drake. Oil painting on wood
by Tan Brunet*

Tan's most recent painting depicts a pair of stately Canvasbacks.

The wood used by most Cajun carvers is tupelo gum. It grows in the swamps and only the bole or immersed part of the tree is suitable for carving. The wood is plentiful, although collecting it entails going out into the swamps and working 'up to the armpits in snakes and alligators' to cut it out. Once dry, the wood has a whitish colour, is light in weight and carves beautifully, seeming to have little or no grain. Traditionally, older decoys were made of the roots of cypress trees which also grow in the swamps. These were frequently blown down by hurricanes, leaving

The swamps of Louisiana yield tupelo and cypress wood,
both ideal for making decoys. The swamps are also full of
snakes and alligators, as I found when I went to photograph
the trees growing in the swamp. The snake in the centre of
the picture tested my resolve as an intrepid photographer,
when I almost trod on it

the roots exposed. This wood is also extremely light in weight.

Not all Louisiana carvers are Cajuns. Many others carve to a very high standard and in various styles. One of the most respected carvers in the state is a young man, William Hanneman, who has found inspiration in the very distinctive decoys of the South. He carves superb decoy style decoratives which capture the classic Louisiana style. He often uses the same wood, cypress root, to stay as close as possible to the Louisiana tradition. His work is remarkably appealing, decorative and collectable.

Louisiana carvers have a very active association, The Louisiana Wildfowl Carvers and Collectors Guild. Every year during September, the annual LWCCG Show and Competition is held at the University of New Orleans. It attracts carvers and artists from all over the state and beyond. The competition is keen with a very high standard in all classes. One of the highlights of the show is the head whittling competition when carvers have two hours in which to carve a duck head. At the same time a decoy painting competition provides plenty of entertainment for the large crowds who flock to the show. There are competitions also at this show for waterfowl painters and photographers and the event concludes with a decoy auction.

Tupelo tree on left growing in the Louisiana swamp. Note the swollen base which yields the wood suitable for carving. The cypress tree on the right has a buttressed shape at the base

William Hanneman

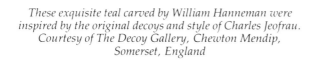

These exquisite teal carved by William Hanneman were
inspired by the original decoys and style of Charles Jeofrau.
Courtesy of The Decoy Gallery, Chewton Mendip,
Somerset, England

Philip J. Galatas — one of Louisiana's most gifted carver artists, pictured here with his wife at the Easton Waterfowl Festival. His pair of Carolina Wood Ducks won top honours at the 1987 New Orleans show

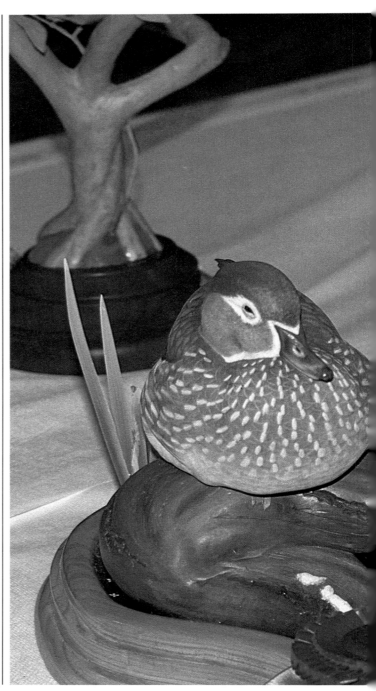

THE BROADER SCENE

Five-day courses at the Decoy Art Studio of Decorative Decoy Carving at Farrington Gurney, England teach beginners the basic techniques of carving, texturing and painting a decorative decoy

My favourite English pigeon decoy! It is more than fifty
years old, is simply yet beautifully carved and was painted
with considerable skill. It has screw eyes and the beak
appears to have been forged from mild steel, perhaps by a
village blacksmith. Collection of the author

Rich areas of decoy history are to be found in the Carolinas, New Jersey, New England, Illinois, California and Canada. To see prime examples of decoys from all regions, a visit to the Shelburne Museum in Vermont is well worth while. The Shelburne is situated a few miles south of the town of Burlington, on the shores of Lake Champlain, about a four hour drive north-west of Boston, through some spectacular Vermont countryside. A good time to arrange your visit to the museum is during the fall, when you will be able to enjoy the legendary glories of the autumnal colours of the trees.

The Shelburne Museum is a large complex covering several acres, and includes a lighthouse and the paddle steamer *Ticonderoga*. The Museum contains large collections of American artefacts and folk art. The decoy collection is the finest in America on public view; it is housed in an early American farm house – the Dorset House. The collection has been built up over many years and includes the original collection of Joel Barber. Here you may see classic decoys by such renowned makers as A. Elmer Crowell, 'Shang' Wheeler, Joe Lincoln, the Ward brothers, Charles Walker and a host of others. A visit to the Shelburne is not something to be rushed – allow yourself at least a day, preferably two, to do it justice.

The Peabody Museum at Salem, Massachusetts, has a relatively small but good collection of decoys by Massachusetts carvers, including a superb collection of miniatures by Elmer Crowell, Joe Lincoln and Alan J. King of North Scituate, Rhode Island. The Crowell and Lincoln miniatures are simply scaled-down versions of their working decoys. The miniatures by Alan King, on the other hand, are carvings which portray the ducks realistically and as they were carved in the 1930s, they are exciting forerunners of what was to follow. I thought them quite exquisite.

If you are visiting any part of America, it is worth asking about decoys in local museums; many have decoys from the region among the items on display. Likewise, it pays to enquire about local decoy competitions and shows; I have been fortunate enough to chance upon a number of such worthwhile events during my travels.

Canada has produced many fine carvers and decoys. Research into Canadian decoy history was

slow to develop but in recent years several well-researched books have been published, revealing a wealth of new interest. Decorative decoy carving flourishes from coast to coast, as in the United States, and there are a number of Canadian carver artists who consistently win at the major competitions. Of these, the best known for his superb work and string of World Championships, is Pat Godin, from Ontario. Pat won his first World Championship in 1976, at the age of 23 and since then, has seldom been out of the limelight. He brings to his work not only artistic and technical ability but also originality in composition and presentation that keep him among the leaders in decoy art. It is interesting to observe the impact of his work on crowds attending the World Championships at Ocean City. 'Stunned silence' probably sums up the reaction of most, gazing in wonder at the perfection of design, detail and workmanship that typifies his work. An honours B.Sc. degree in Wildlife Biology from Guelph University, Ontario, followed by an M.Sc. degree based on research into Mallard ecology, backed by considerable practical work with waterfowl, gives Pat an unrivalled expertise in all aspects of waterfowl knowledge. It is this which is reflected in his work and gives it such assertion. Pat has also been active in teaching, conducting practical carving seminars across America and instructing through video courses. He has recently published two excellent pattern and instruction books which provide invaluable and reliable information to decoy carvers.

Decoy art has crossed the oceans like a seed on the wind and has settled in very fertile soil in Britain. Since 1984 there has been a School of Decorative Decoy Carving at Farrington Gurney in Somerset: over 1500 students have attended its courses. Courses have also been held at centres of The Wildfowl Trust and Royal Society for the Protection of Birds (RSPB) and at the Natural History Museum in London. Two competitions have so far been held in Britain and while yet on a small scale as compared to America – as might be expected – they have, nevertheless, been well attended. Recently, a fine new gallery has opened which will specialise in decoys. The Decoy Gallery at Chewton Mendip, near Bath, Somerset, will enable the public to see the work of contemporary American and British decoy makers

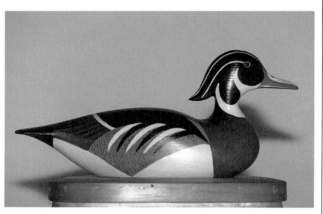

This excellent replica of the classic Joe Lincoln Wood Duck drake decoy (pictured on p.155) was made by Judith Nicholl, one of Britain's new up and coming decoy carvers. Courtesy of The Decoy Gallery

along with some antique decoys. It will help foster the art form in Britain by giving up-and-coming decoy artists an opportunity to exhibit and sell their work in ideal surroundings.

Elsewhere, there is at least one keen duck carver, Arthur Reid, in Iceland and growing numbers of enthusiasts in mainland Europe. In South Africa, Jo Wicht has been carving decoys for several years and finds that people there respond enthusiastically to her work. There is considerable interest in New

LEFT: Simple decoy style carvings can give immense satisfaction to a beginner. This Mallard drake by the author was one of his earliest carvings

BELOW: This magnificent preening Pintail drake by World Champion Pat Godin, of Ontario, Canada, demonstrates his wonderful mastery of all aspects of decorative decoy art

Zealand and Australia; Dr Hugh Lavery of Brisbane, Australia, has been discovering exciting examples of decoys used for hunting in Australia and the Far East. There is growing interest in Japan, and Ma Hai Feng from Hong Kong is a regular prizewinner at 'the World' competition. It is only a matter of time before the art form is truly international.

I am often asked about the likelihood of there being undiscovered old decoys indigenous to Europe. There are some, perhaps, but so far research has been disappointing. Some have been traced in France, a few in Holland, a few in Scandinavia, but nothing yet suggests anything to get excited about. Time will tell but I have no great hopes of anything remarkable appearing. It is well known that pigeon decoys were widely used in Britain and from time to time attractively carved examples come to light, although the majority are fairly rudimentary. They have been keenly sought by dealers in recent years and many have gone to collectors in America.

COLLECTING

Decoys are extremely attractive and desirable objects and, once bitten by the bug, collecting them can become an obsession. I have asked many people why they collect decoys. Answers have ranged from 'They look good around the home', 'They are a part of American history and they remind me of the old days', 'They remind me of hunting', to 'I think they are a good investment', and, of course, combinations of all of these.

Decoys certainly do look good around the house. Most people who have become aware of decoys recently, particularly in Europe, have done so because decoys are now frequently to be seen in the interiors depicted in glossy 'home' magazines. They are also often to be seen in film and television sets. Certainly they are to be found in many middle-class American homes and 'preppy' lawyers, doctors and businessmen often have a brace in the office. We are talking here of 'real' decoys, not the mass-produced 'cheap and cheerful' ducks that are to be seen in shops everywhere. If you want to get it right, your decoy should be 'the real McCoy'. Ideally you should know the name of the maker and where it came from. It is fine to have picked one up whilst strolling along the side of a lake in Canada, or wherever you went on holiday, 15 years ago. Then there is a touch of mystery to add romance to your wooden bird – it might just be the work of a famous maker and worth a fortune.

Decoys as decor have a lot going for them. They can be moved around by just picking them up and trying them in new locations with much less bother than pictures. They look good anywhere in the house, on the floor, on mantelpieces or shelves and in cabinets. Visitors find decoys fascinating and they invariably generate discussion. A cautionary word here if you have a dog. It must be said that dogs find gnawing on a decoy only marginally less pleasing than a bone. You will often find descriptions in catalogues like this one from a large decoy auction in 1986: 'Canada Goose: condition: old repaint shows average wear. Several age splits. Bill has been partially chewed by a dog.' There are several such descriptions in the same catalogue. Of course, dogs are used for hunting and this damage may have been inflicted during active service. It is not so amusing when the bird has been brought home and placed in

Part of Captain Jimmy Vizier's collection displayed
decoratively in his home

your collection. I shall not easily forget once finding my Labrador puppy in the livingroom looking very pleased with himself, surrounded by the chewed remains of a valuable shore bird decoy. The description 'Lightly hit by shot' on the other hand, is a much more acceptable, even desirable, flaw, proving that at least your decoy has seen active service.

Decoys certainly evoke a feeling of place and history. As I look at decoys in my own modest collection, they are a reminder of the places where they originated and, as many of them are by contemporary carvers, whom I know well, they remind me of happy times spent visiting them. Old decoys of unknown origin are fascinating because it is so interesting trying to discover who made them and when. Sometimes there is a clue as to the area where it was made, which may eventually lead to discovering the maker. Some time ago I purchased a pair of flying ducks of a type that were sometimes made by decoy makers for sporting goods stores or maybe as decoration for a gunning club. The vendor had no idea where they had come from or who had made them. They appear to be made by different carvers – in style they are quite different – yet they are clearly a drake and duck (hen). How did they come together? The drake is particularly well carved and has a certain dignity that leads me to believe he is by a 'quality' carver. They are almost certainly American in origin – what brought them to Britain? The eyes of the drake are incised into the head, then painted over. This clue points in the direction of the Long Island area, where carvers like Obadiah Verity of Seaford used this method to fashion eyes. Could it be the work of the great man himself? Such quests can be really exciting.

There are not many really old decoys about; most in collections were made in this century so it has been possible for researchers in recent years to uncover a lot of information from family recollection, from old photographs and documents such as account books. Much more is known today about decoys and their makers than when Joel Barber wrote *Wild Fowl Decoys* in 1934. Most of the research was done by region and has been published in book form so that regional decoy history is recorded in often minute detail.

Many collectors are hunters to whom a decoy is a symbol of enjoyable times spent out on the marshes,

waiting in the hide for the wild duck to fly into the rig. Add to this the camaraderie of good companions, the excitement and the pleasure of being in the open air close to nature and I can readily understand this symbolism. Even though not a hunter myself, I nevertheless do find excitement in simply seeing the wild birds flying into a well deployed rig of decoys. Many decoy carvers like to do this to observe more closely ducks and geese.

Collecting decoys as a financial investment is an attractive idea when one considers the track record of the past ten years. When I first became interested in decoys in the late seventies the record price paid for a single decoy at auction stood at $10,500. In May 1986 I went to Hyannis in Massachusetts to the Richard A. Bourne auction house, where a decoy from the collection of the late Dr George Starr, author of *Decoys of the Atlantic Flyway*, was expected to breach the $100,000 level for the first time. Collectors and decoy enthusiasts from all over America were there and the excitement was intense. The decoy involved was one of hundreds being auctioned from the Starr collection and was a fine and rare Carolina Wood Duck drake by Massachusetts decoy carver Joe Lincoln. Bidding for the bird started high and continued briskly up to the $100,000 level; on up to $200,000 to be knocked down eventually at a price of $205,000! Later that year a preening Pintail decoy by another Massachusetts maker, A. Elmer Crowell, shattered that record by selling for $319,000. It seemed incredible that within the space of less than ten years the record price could have multiplied to such a level – even *The Wall Street Journal* took note by reporting the event. This record still stands.

Be it understood that these are outstanding and rare decoys and represent spectacular prices far above the general level. Yet even so, the price level of decoys generally has risen dramatically in recent years. The word is that many of the big prices are paid by investment companies, who see in decoys plenty of scope for improvement as collecting increases in popularity and more people become interested in the subject. Remember that decoys are still relatively unknown outside America. Who knows what might happen if the big guns in the art world take a liking to decoys? A third of a million dollars sounds a lot of money but compared to prices paid for paintings by artists like Van Gogh, it is small

ABOVE: *The beautiful and rare Wood Duck drake by Massachusetts decoy maker, Joe Lincoln. Photograph by courtesy of Richard A Bourne Co. Inc. Hyannis Port, Massachusetts*

BELOW: *The world record price preening Pintail decoy by Massachusetts maker A. Elmer Crowell. Photograph by Ellen Meserve courtesy of Richard W. Oliver Auction Gallery, Kennebunk, Maine*

change. My own hunch is that decoys will continue to increase in price and the day of the one million dollar decoy is not too far away. Time will tell.

So how can a newcomer to decoy collecting make a start? Naturally that depends very much on how much money he has available. It is so easy to wring one's hands and say 'If only I had been around ten/fifteen years ago.' Yet I believe there are just as many good opportunities now as there were then. You can still find very collectable old decoys in the $200-$1000 price range. There are some excellent contemporary carvers producing fine work which may well appreciate in value if the market generally improves. The work of many of the carvers mentioned in this book, and many more besides, are already collected by people who have been successful in spotting winners. Many of the contemporary carvers have long waiting lists for this very reason – collectors are queueing up to buy their work.

The would-be decoy collector outside North America may feel at a disadvantage, being so far from the source of most of the world's finest decoys. However, this may not be the case. I have been told many times in America that decoys were shipped in large numbers overseas – many to Europe, some to South America and other places where waterfowl were hunted. Because decoy collecting is as yet virtually unknown outside America, many people elsewhere may possess decoys and be unaware of their potential value, even, at times, what they are. Some time ago I was interviewed on national radio here in Britain about my School of Decorative Decoy Carving and on decoys in general. The next day I received a telephone call from a lady who said that she had 12 pairs of 'funny little wooden ducks' and could I tell her what they might be. They turned out to be a lovely collection of miniature decoys by the late Captain Jesse Urie, a well-known decoy maker, of Rockhall, Maryland. As such, they had a considerable value, which came as a great surprise to the lady who had owned them for many years, quite unaware that they were anything special.

If you are going into collecting old decoys it will pay to do some reading first, to decide which areas and types of decoy interest you most. It is extremely good experience to go to one or two auctions where you can see all the decoys to be sold before the auction starts. You will find other people most helpful in pointing out to you things that may not be obvious. For instance does the decoy have its original paint (often noted as 'OP' in dealers' lists and catalogues)? This greatly enhances a decoy's value. Auction houses do their best to describe decoys as accurately as possible and most have experienced assessors who know their subject well. If the authenticity of a decoy can be proved to be false, most auction houses will refund the purchase price subject to the refund being made within a certain stipulated time period.

If you are unable to travel to America to attend an auction, nearly all of them will accept telephone bids. Most of the beautiful – often quite expensive – auction catalogues contain superb photographs of many of the decoys and you could buy your bird that way.

Even if you are buying in order to speculate, always buy a decoy that you actually like the look of. That way you can get enjoyment from your investment, even if it doesn't make you rich.

There are plenty of dealers who can help you find what you are looking for. Many specialise in decoys of a certain type or from certain areas. Quite a few of the dealers are top authorities in the field; some have written authoritative books on the decoys of their area.

There are pitfalls to watch out for in buying decoys, as with anything else. 'Let the buyer beware' is as sound advice now as when the Romans first introduced the legal principle 2,000 years ago. There are certainly some forged decoys around. Some are so cleverly done that they have fooled even experts. Ward brothers decoys seem to be a favourite target for forgers. Someone I know even has a collection of Ward forgeries! It is, of course, perfectly in order to carve a replica of a favourite classic decoy – I have done so myself – as long as it is not done to deceive others.

There are many 'if only' stories in decoy collecting. The manager of a motel where I was staying once on a visit to the Eastern Shore, told me how he had once found seven Ward brothers decoys on a rubbish tip. He thought he would try using them for hunting instead of the plastic ones he normally used. He had two of them repainted by Lem Ward and 'they came up like new', he told me. 'I intended to get Lem to paint up the rest,' he went on, 'but somehow I never

RIGHT: *This superb pair of Red Breasted merganser decoys with raised wing detail and inletted heads are by an unknown maker from Monhegan Island, Maine. They represent decoy folk art at its finest*

BELOW: *Part of the fabulous collection of Ward Brothers decoys belonging to collectors 'Mort' and Carol Kramer. Photograph by the author courtesy of Dr and Mrs Morton Kramer*

got around to it. Next I heard he had died and that was that.'

The final tragedy in this sad tale was even worse. 'Then my wife and I split up and she took the decoys with her.'

Decoy collectors on a grand scale are Dr Morton Kramer and his wife Carol. Their spacious and elegant home is full of superb decoys. How many exactly, they are not sure, but it is certainly hundreds, if not thousands. Most are by the Ward brothers, some by Oliver Lawson and the rest by Mark McNair.

They started their collection in 1961. A friend introduced them to the Ward brothers in Crisfield and they developed a warm friendship with the brothers, visiting them and buying a decoy whenever they could. Their visits were always enjoyable, they loved listening to the stories the brothers told and were excited every time they added another decoy to their collection. 'Yet it was something more than that which attracted us to the Wards,' says Dr Kramer. 'We were aware that something significant and extraordinary was happening. Although the Wards denigrated themselves, we

knew that they had genius.'

They collected Ward decoys because they liked them, they were interested in hunting and enjoyed the decoys around the house. They bought the decoys at whatever the going rate happened to be and certainly had no thought of their growing collection as a financial investment.

Dr Kramer remembers how the Wards were keen to sell miniatures at one time because they had decided to put a bathroom into their house. 'Generally they had not much interest in money, although I think they were impressed when their work started to command high prices. What did upset them somewhat, was when we started to buy some of their earlier work second-hand, when they thought we could have bought *new* ones from them direct!'

The Kramers also have a great deal of Ward brothers memorabilia, including letters, photographs, press cuttings and some of the old tools and equipment they used in their carving. They are wonderfully knowledgeable about decoys generally and especially the decoys in their collection. They often attend shows such as the Easton Waterfowl Festival,

Duck stamp designs are usually selected by competition. Winning can bring fame and fortune to successful artists. Here Jude Brunet, younger son of World Champion decoy carver Tan Brunet, is seen with a duck stamp design he was working on during my visit

taking along part of their collection to share with other enthusiasts.

Decoy enthusiasts do not confine their collecting to decoys alone. Among special interest items collected are decoy weights, auction catalogues, posters of shows, festivals, and competitions, duck calls (instrument used to provide a quacking sound), the Easton Waterfowl Festival annual handbook, decoy books, duck stamps and prints, and decoy makers' signs – indeed anything related to the subject. Many of these items have become so popular that they now change hands at prices considerably above their original value.

'Duck stamps' in particular have developed into a highly specialised area of collection. What are duck stamps? They are annual hunting licence fee stamps, issued either by the US Federal authorities as a levy to provide funds to control hunting and to help with conservation or by state authorities for the same purpose. Competitions are held to select suitable designs for the stamps annually, the selected artists winning publicity and great prestige thereby and the right to publish prints of their artwork. Since inception, the design subject has generally been waterfowl – hence the name 'duck stamps', although fish and other subjects are now often depicted. The state of Massachusetts chose to illustrate its stamps with pictures of decoys carved by Massachusetts decoy makers. The result is a series of extremely attractive stamps depicting, among others, such fine decoys as the Joe Lincoln Wood duck, which set the new world record auction price in 1986. Most prints are issued as limited editions; once sold out, they find their value level in the secondary (second-hand) market and certain popular prints have rocketed in price. It is usual to frame the print with the actual 'duck stamp' set below the picture, making an extremely attractive picture to hang on the wall. The State of Maryland honoured the Ward brothers with a special duck stamp in 1980, painted by artist Jack Schroeder, depicting the brothers and one of their pintail decoys. As might be expected, this proved to be very popular with decoy enthusiasts.

Not to be confused with the 'duck stamps' described above, the US Postal Authority issued a set of four mail postage stamps, depicting decoys, on 22 March 1985. First day covers from Shelburne, home

Massachusetts 'duck stamps' depict decoys made by Massachusetts carvers. Here are two of the series of these attractive and very collectable stamps

Decoy weights come in a wide variety of shapes and sizes
and make interesting 'collectables'. I found this selection
in a corner of Chincoteague carver Roe 'Ducman' Terry's
workshop and he kindly allowed me to photograph them.
As Roe is a hunting guide who uses decoys, these weights
are still in active service

The attractively designed Chincoteague Easter Decoy Festival posters by local artist Hal Lott have become very popular with collectors. By courtesy of The Decoy Gallery, Chewton Mendip, Somerset, England.

of the famous decoy museum, were greatly in demand and the stamps proved to be very popular with the American public. Some decoy experts questioned the selection of the particular decoys depicted but generally the decoy fraternity welcomed the stamps as an indication of general public awareness of the place of decoys as true American folk art.

Duck calls make an attractive collecting speciality. It is not generally recognised outside America how important and integral a part of hunting, and how complementary to decoying, duck calling is. Certainly a large proportion of American duck hunters make a good job of duck calling and the holding of competitions and championships helps to hone these skills. Typically, duck and goose calling competitions play to full houses, with standing room only at the back and they are wonderfully entertaining events to attend. Some of the contenders even manage without a reed call, using just their voices. One of the best known of them is a lady caller who seems to have a spellbinding hold over audiences, agog at her remarkable skill. A duck or goose call finished in fine wood such as walnut, with maybe silver or sometimes gold inlays, can be an attractive object, as can a simpler one made by some old-timer from way back.

Of late, fish decoys have come very popular with collectors. Probably the rapid escalation in duck decoy prices has had some effect in making collectors at the lower price levels turn to the more affordable fish decoys. In fact, fish decoys can be extremely appealing objects. Just as duck decoys have led to the carving of decorative decoys, so has the interest in fish decoys led to a new surge of interest among carvers to carve decorative fish. Decorative fish carving is not, however, totally new and unheard of. The great New England decoy maker, 'Shang' Wheeler, carved superb and beautifully detailed trout and salmon as long ago as 1910. These may be seen illustrated in the excellent book *Shang*, by Dixon MacD. Merkt with Mark H. Lytle.

So how and where were fish decoys used? In many of the northern (sometimes called 'ice box') states of America and in Canada, lakes freeze over in winter to the extent that it is quite safe to move about on the ice. Fishermen found themselves a place on the ice, constructed a hut, then cut out a hole in the ice

Fish decoy with metal fins and internal lead ballast weight

By courtesy of The Decoy Gallery,
Chewton Mendip, Somerset, England

through which to fish. The hut was primarily as protection from the elements but also to block the light and make it easier to see into the water beneath the ice. Fish decoys were suspended through the hole and ballasted so as to drop down easily into the depths below. A spear with five or six pronged barbs on it was used to strike the quarry when it appeared within sight and range, attracted it was hoped, by the fish decoys. These could be manipulated and jiggled by the hunter to attract attention and improve their realism. Often the tail fin, usually made of sheet metal, was bent to promote circular swimming actions when the decoy was manoeuvred. Fishermen often stayed in their huts for days at a time, fishing in this way and could sometimes be rewarded by a huge fish, maybe a big sturgeon or muskie. So popular was this sport that whole townships of huts could be seen on some lakes. This suggests that there might be vast numbers of fish decoys waiting to be discovered by collectors. Already the prices being made by these hitherto-unsought-after decoys indicate that demand for them will rise rapidly.

DECOY ART

RIGHT: *Yellowleg shorebird decoy by Mark McNair*

By 1965 decoys had become recognised as a uniquely American folk art. Collectors were beginning to scour the country looking for decoys and researching the lives of the men who made them. At this time it was possible to go out and find decoys which could be acquired for just a few dollars.

Such a collector was William Mackey, who wrote the book *American Bird Decoys*, which became for many years a standard reference book. Just as Joel Barber's book had excited interest in 1934, the Mackey book triggered a new surge of interest.

The label 'folk art' seemed to give decoys a new dignity and value. Even people who had grown up surrounded by decoys, which hitherto they had barely noticed, started to observe them differently.

The question has been raised, 'Is folk art a valid description for artefacts or pieces of equipment which were made solely and intentionally for hunting?'

So, what is folk art? Do contemporary decorative decoys qualify as 'fine art'? What indeed is art?

These are difficult questions to answer and the whole subject of definitions in the world of art is something of a minefield.

We may safely say that man alone, of all the animals on this planet, reflects his wonder at what he sees all around him through art. Artistic expression is common to people of all races. All men are capable of artistic expression, even those who may insist and believe that they are not artistic.

If an ordinary person, who has not been trained as an artist, sees a beautiful rose and feels moved to paint a picture of it, is this naive art or folk art? Does it depend on how good a job he makes of the painting and, if so, who is to be the judge of that?

The question is, if decoys were made as tools of the hunt, can they be folk art? If so, might not fishing boats, which are intended for fishing, yet have beautiful lines and are often brightly coloured, also be considered folk art – or are they something to do with craft?

Perhaps it is our decorative perception of decoys that turns them into art. The moment I bring a decoy – a simple hunting tool – into my home and place it on a shelf where I may enjoy looking at it along with other decorative objects such as pottery, pictures and so on, it becomes decorative art. If my home were large enough to accommodate it and if I could afford to buy one, I think a brightly painted Greek fishing boat would be a wonderful piece of art to collect. So is it the folk who made them or the folk who perceive them as decorative art, who are the folk in folk art?

The attitude of the maker must have some bearing on the argument. Many decoy makers chopped out decoys day after day, all to the same pattern, and they simply represented so much cash when they were sold. There is not much soul in that! On the other hand, someone like Lem Ward fashioned a humble working decoy, yet imparted to his work something that was a reflection of the glory of God's creation as he perceived it all around him. That attitude surely makes his work art.

For myself, I find little difficulty in accepting the term 'folk art' as applied to hand made wooden hunting decoys and have even less difficulty in accepting the term 'fine art' to describe the work of contemporary decorative decoy artists at the highest level. Given the refinement of its execution, the meticulous attention to anatomical detail and painting and the compositional presentation, it is most certainly art and definitely fine.

In using such terms, are we getting close to the rarified atmosphere of art galleries, art critics and precious attitudes here? Happily not. The world of decoy art seems to be inhabited by very uncomplicated people who are not given to pretentious humbug. The fresh air of the seashore and marshes, of the bayous and lakes, ventilates the world of decoy art in a most refreshing way.

It is interesting to note that the great majority of decorative decoy artists have had no formal art training. A number of professional carvers do run courses of instruction which usually last for no more than a week. There are a number of good books of instruction in wildfowl carving and painting. Clubs and associations across America bring carvers together as, of course, do competitions, where there is always a great deal of information exchanged on techniques.

I have been impressed by the open-handed way in which experienced carvers will give guidance and advice quite freely to the beginner attending his first show. It says something of the wide appeal and indeed the addictive nature of this art form, that so

many people not only start it but persevere until they become very good at it.

The benefits of this are manifold. Not only is decoy art a delightfully therapeutic occupation for the hobby carver, it is awakening the interest of thousands of ordinary people to the beauty of our wild birds and the need to preserve them and their habitat from the truly dreadful things which are destroying so much of this planet. It may even be a subconscious reaction to this growing crisis that has resulted in this remarkable response to decoy art, by carvers and collectors alike. Perhaps the duck on the mantelpiece is a symbolic reminder of the wild duck struggling to survive and raise its young on water poisoned by industrial waste and acid rain.

It is something of a paradox that even in its fine art form, decorative decoy art is still a folk art, using the term 'folk' here in the sense of 'ordinary people' as opposed to trained artists. It draws people from a very broad spectrum of society; there seem to be just as many women carvers as men and of all ages. That so many people are now actively concerned with colour, form and texture raises the hope that we may be moving away from the plastic age towards a modern renaissance. There is another reason, I believe, why decoy art is growing so rapidly in popularity. The majority of ordinary people cannot easily relate to modern abstract art. Apart from a small percentage of sophisticates who claim understanding and enjoyment of it, most people feel such art to be rather pointless, indeed many feel they are being conned. Whether they are or not doesn't matter, the suspicion is there. On the other hand, decoy art represents a return at last to 'honest art'. There is no doubt what is going on here. People can relate immediately to the subject; they can understand – even marvel at – the skill required to accomplish the work and they respect the discipline and study which the artist had to bring to his work. And they do so automatically without anyone having to persuade them with pretentious 'art speak'.

Two things occurred in 1970 which were to give decorative decoy carving a new impetus and direction. An ambitious new annual competition was held for the first time. This was the World Championship Wildfowl Carving Competition held at Ocean City. The title 'World Championship' was ambitious, because at that time there was little competition likely to come from outside America. Yet the World Championship it became, and as events have developed, this was perfectly justified; competition from overseas is already evident and will surely grow as decoy art spreads worldwide.

Perhaps even more significant than this was a breakthrough in carving technique. A clergyman carver from New Mexico, the Reverend Jack Drake, hit on an idea to produce realistic-looking feathers on his carvings. By using an electrically heated burning tool with a sharp edge, he burned fine lines representing feathers on his ducks. A feather looks like a feather because of the way the barbs reflect the light. By creating a similar light reflective surface, remarkable realism could be achieved. Hitherto feather effects had been painted on to decorative birds, such birds being known nowadays as 'slicks'.

The shock waves of Jack Drake's new technique echoed round the decoy carving world. Suddenly, total realism was the name of the game. The early feather texturing tools were somewhat crude but it was not long before tools capable of achieving very fine results were on the market. Decoy carving as a hobby was becoming so popular that a support industry supplying tools, materials and instruction books, was developing rapidly. It was quick to respond to new demands.

By the mid-to late 1970s, feather burning and the insertion of feathers in wing construction was giving rise to ambitious pieces in which every feather was defined. Many carvers were not happy with this new direction, calling it model building, not carving. They felt it was getting away from the original spirit of decoy carving. Through judicious shaping of the competition rules the Ward Foundation managed to keep a reasonable balance. Hunting decoys remained a firm part of most competitions and although 'decoy art' now embraces nearly every species of bird, ducks continue to constitute a high proportion of every World Championship and this has continued to the present time.

In the late 1970s the setting of bird carvings into their habitat became a feature which added a new dimension of realism. It allowed composition to play a part in the overall artistic effect. Moreover, the carver artist had to research the habitat and match it to the bird depicted – a bird in winter plumage had to be set in the appropriate winter habitat. In such set

LEFT: *This dramatic carving of a snake threatening a group of birds aroused great interest at the 1987 World Championships*

RIGHT: *This delightful small songbird carving is by talented Louisiana carver Fredi Bowen. Fredi and her husband Gene produce exquisite duck, bird and fish carvings*

pieces, structural engineering sometimes plays a large part in the dramatic effect produced. Often birds were shown in a flying position, the whole weight of the wooden bird being borne on a single feather contact to the main structure.

In the 1987 World Championship a dramatic carving, depicting a snake threatening a group of birds, pleased the crowds enormously. To my knowledge this was the first time a snake had entered the field of decoy art. Pat Godin had introduced a muskrat in his brilliant 'Best in World' set piece 'Along the Grand', a few years before and likewise that had enormous

impact. Fish carvings have also increased in popularity of late and at the 1987 Easton Waterfowl Festival some carvings of weather-worn rocks had a powerful impact. It would appear from these signs, that 'decoy art' may be entering an exciting new stage in which artists will be able to represent nature in total realism in a way that has never been done before. The techniques are certainly there; it is fundamentally no more difficult, in terms of technique, to carve a leopard than a duck. My guess is that decoy art will develop along these lines – it will certainly be exciting to see!

HOW A DECORATIVE DECOY
IS MADE

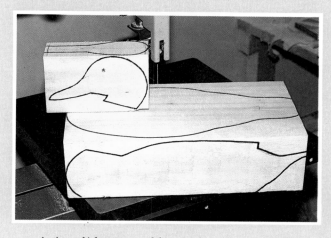

*A piece of jelutong wood from Malaya is marked with the
pattern of the duck, a full-sized Mallard drake. These two
profiles are then cut out on a bandsaw*

RIGHT: *The tools of the trade. Decoys can be carved using simple hand tools. On our courses students carve their first duck using just the simple Stanley craft knife and sandpaper*

BELOW: *This superbly illustrated wallchart of diving and dabbling ducks by leading waterfowl artist, Hilary Burn, is very popular with decorative decoy carvers*

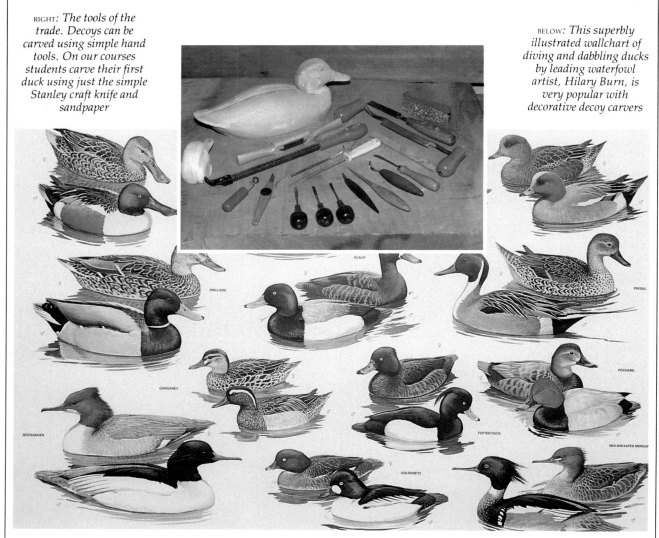

It is possible that what you have seen and read in this book so far will have made you interested to know how a decorative decoy is made. It has been my pleasure, during recent years, to help hundreds of people, from all over Britain and many other parts of the world, to carve their first duck at our school in Somerset. Nearly all were absolute beginners, new to carving, to feather texturing and to painting. Yet at the end of an intensive five-day course, all went away with a beautiful duck. This was usually a Mallard drake, with shimmering iridescent green and blue head and many subtly blended colours. Many of these people have since told me that when they arrived home with their ducks, their families and friends were astonished at what they had achieved. Quite a high proportion of these beginners have now developed into fine carvers; indeed, some have even turned professional and now sell their work successfully.

At first sight, carving and painting a beautiful duck may seem a difficult task; something that only the very capable and talented can do. But if that task is broken down into a series of simple steps, taken one at a time, each step on its own does not seem so difficult.

Don't expect your first duck to be a masterpiece. Do your best, be prepared to make some mistakes – learn from them and keep on practising. Practice is as important in decoy carving as it is in playing the violin or any other skill.

I believe that the cornerstone of good decoy carving is observation. Before you even think of picking up a piece of wood and a knife, you have to learn as much as possible about ducks. If you are new to ducks, you will need to recognise the different types. Some are divers, some dabblers, that is

BELOW: *At this stage the head should be checked for symmetry and correct proportion*

BELOW RIGHT: *It is tremendously satisfying to hollow decoys although not strictly necessary for a decorative carving. Using a 1" Forstner pattern drill in a drill press, a series of holes are drilled as illustrated. Both bottom plate surfaces must be planed flat to make a perfect joint when glued together*

The drilled-out space may be hollowed out further, either with hand tools or, in this case, using the reciprocating chisel of the Japanese Automach tool, followed by the rotary action Karbide Kutzall rasps used in the same tool. The reciprocating and rotary handpieces illustrated are connected to the machine by a 39" flexidrive shaft. This wonder tool from Japan has been eagerly adopted by decoy carvers, as it performs such a variety of functions with great efficiency

The bottom plate has been glued on and the final shaping leaves a fine glue line just visible. When glueing the bottom on, drop a small wood chip or a dried bean inside, so that when shaken it is possible to hear that the decoy is hollow

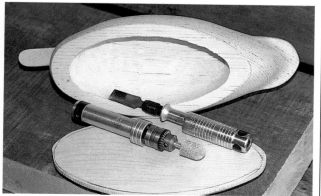

surface feeders that 'upend' to feed (sometimes called marsh ducks). You will note that they are quite different in shape; the divers are much rounder than the more peardrop-shaped dabblers. Note also the difference in their tails and the different position of the legs. There are quite a few species, but you will soon learn to identify them with the aid of a good wallchart or identification book. Then you will need to concentrate on a particular species, perhaps the one you plan to carve. Start to note its colours and special features. What colour are the eyes? What shape is the bill? Answering these and many more questions will eventually enable you to carve a realistic-looking duck. Fortunately, watching ducks is very enjoyable and sooner or later you will be inspired to carve a particular type of duck. Now that we know which duck we are going to carve, we can start by making the pattern.

The first consideration is the size of the bird in relation to the thickness of the wood available. Will it be necessary to laminate? To laminate means joining two pieces of wood together to make a larger block. For example, a full-sized Canada Goose will need two pieces of 4" thick wood laminated together to make up the blank for the body. This involves planing two surfaces flat, then glueing the pieces together. You may wish to hollow your duck. This again needs consideration at the pattern stage. Most full-size ducks fit into a 4" thick piece of wood. If you have only 3" thick stock and don't like the idea of planing and glueing two pieces of wood together, then you can reduce the size of your duck accordingly.

Any object with space all around it is said to be three-dimensional. As such, it can be expressed graphically in three drawings which can be described as the end profile, the side profile and the top profile.

LEFT: *Method of drawing the pattern*

RIGHT: *The bandsawn blank has two of the three profiles already established. People often refer to these blanks as 'roughed out' shapes. This is not particularly apt as the bandsaw operator follows the pattern lines accurately to establish these profiles. Provided the carver does not cut within these profiles, he will end up with a duck of the same shape as the one he drew in the original pattern.*

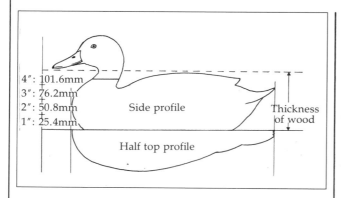

4": 101.6mm
3": 76.2mm
2": 50.8mm
1": 25.4mm

Side profile

Thickness of wood

Half top profile

The pattern is made by drawing on a suitable piece of paper, a large letter T on its side. Let us say, in this instance, that we have 4" thick wood. Measure up from the base line 4". A line is now drawn parallel to the base line as indicated. This represents the side profile of our block of wood. Now the side profile of the duck is drawn within that wood thickness. The head is drawn as well to get the proportions right, although the head will come from a separate piece of wood.

Perpendiculars are now dropped from the ends of the duck's side profile. Within those lines are drawn in a half top profile of the duck, from the base line down. The half profile is drawn so that we may be sure of a symmetrical whole top profile by turning over the half on the other side of the centre line.

The block of wood is now marked up using a soft black lead pencil, after which it is ready to be bandsawn.

A bandsaw consists of an electric motor, driving by pulley two wheels set vertically one above the other, around which a continuous loop blade is placed. The teeth of the blade cut one way only as the blade descends through a gap in the cutting table. This table is mounted on trunnions to enable it to be angled so that bevelled cuts may be made. The chief advantage of a bandsaw is its ability to make curved cuts as the wood is directed by hand around the blade, which is normally not more than ¾" wide. The tighter the radius of curves being cut, the narrower is the blade fitted, down to ¼" wide.

A bandsaw, like any woodworking machine, can be extremely dangerous if used carelessly, so it is necessary always to adjust the various guards that are fitted, before using the machine. Follow the maker's instructions for tensioning the blade. It is most important for the operator to wear a protective shield for the eyes and to have protection from dust, either with dust-extracting equipment or by wearing an air-filtering mask. Ingested wood dust can cause very unpleasant health problems.

To cut out the blank, the wood is cut first down one side of the top profile until near the middle where the pattern runs about parallel to the side of the block. The blade is then backed out carefully. The other side is cut in the same way. The block is turned and the process repeated on both sides until the inner end of the cut is about ¾" from the opposite cut.

By this method, the side profile pattern has been retained intact, also leaving a flat side to keep the block level as the side profile is cut right around. As the pieces fall away, we see clearly where the side pieces now have to be removed. Then the cutting table is tilted to about 45 degrees and some of the corner of the blank is removed to save time in the carving. This is done 'by eye'.

Bandsaws are expensive and many decoy carvers do not own one, but it is possible to buy bandsawn blanks, either to your own pattern or a standard pattern, from a good decoy materials supplier.

Now the head is cut out, using a similar procedure. The piece of wood removed from beneath the bill is retained, to support the wood whilst making the cuts along the sides of the bill. This prevents the blade 'snatching' at the wood.

The bandsawn blank is now ready for carving. The blank looks remarkably like a duck already: in fact, two-thirds of the shape is already established.

The body and head have been rounded to shape and the tertial feathers have been raised from the body. Slots will be cut beneath these feathers to receive the primary feather inserts. If it is decided to carve the primary feathers integrally with the body, then, of course, extra stock will have to be provided at the bandsawing stage

You will have noticed that ducks are very round in shape, so our first task is to round the body. Beginners are always anxious about taking off too much wood, which usually results in not taking off enough. This is a reasonable enough fear since once wood is removed you cannot put it back. This is where it really becomes necessary to monitor each stage of your work by holding it up in front of you and 'eyeballing' each of those three profiles. If you look at what you are doing in this way, it will be easy to judge where you need to use your knife or tool.

A word here about wood grain. Whatever you use, whether it is a knife, draw knife, axe or any other tool, you will always have to be aware of the direction of the grain of the wood. This is the term used to describe the alignment of the fibrous tubes that carry the water and nutrients – the sap – from the root system to the new growth area where it is needed. The old expression 'going against the grain' describes doing things the hard way. Go with the grain and wood is one of the sweetest materials to work in – fight the grain and you are in trouble. The golden rule is 'always cut downhill across the grain'. On our courses, we always start students off with a little exercise to make this point – we carve an egg. You might care to try this yourself. An egg is quite a demanding thing to carve well. If you can carve an egg, you can certainly carve a duck.

Think of the widest point of the egg as the top of a hill, then carve away from that point downhill on each side.

If the egg shape was expressed by contours as on a map, it would look as here on the right.

A duck on the water has its wings folded; they rest

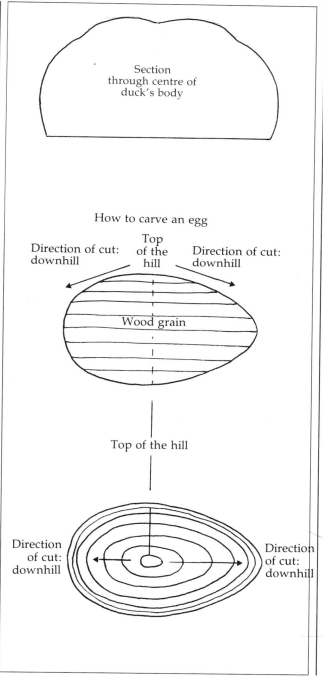

Section through centre of duck's body

How to carve an egg

Direction of cut: downhill   Top of the hill   Direction of cut: downhill

Wood grain

Top of the hill

Direction of cut: downhill   Direction of cut: downhill

RIGHT: *The head is sanded smooth and detail added to the bill. It is very helpful to have a resin-cast study bill from which detail and dimensions may be taken*

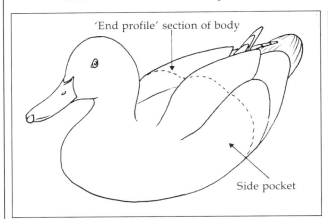

'End profile' section of body

Side pocket

Side view of head showing eye groove and cheek

beside the body and are protected by a group of feathers known as the wing coverts. Duck carvers often refer to this as the side pocket, as if the folded wing were contained within a protective pocket of feathers. This gives the body a contoured shape like this.

The tail of a duck is an area that causes problems for beginners. It must be realised that the tail is a simple fan of feathers that sticks out from the body. Above and below are coverts – the undertail coverts and the upper tail coverts – that streamline the bird in flight. We have to make the tail as thin as the single fan of feathers, yet retain enough strength to avoid breakage. The beginner is probably well advised to keep the tail at least 1/8" thick to start with, gradually thinning down as he or she becomes more confident with the knife. The important thing is to get the tail wrapped around the back end of the duck and of uniform thickness all the way round.

The head is normally carved separately from the body; that way it is easier to work on all the detail around the bill. Also, if the head is to be turned, it enables the grain to be aligned with the bill for maximum strength.

Note the following points:

1   The eye is located in a groove – the eye groove which runs from the point of the culmen towards the rear of the head. Below is the cheek and above the supercilium, a slight overhang.

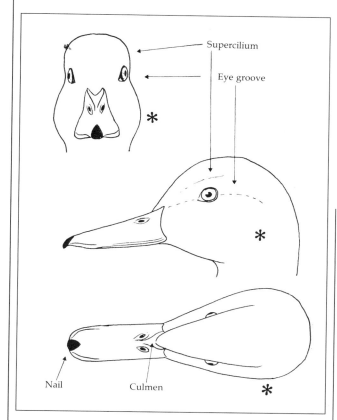

Supercilium

Eye groove

Nail

Culmen

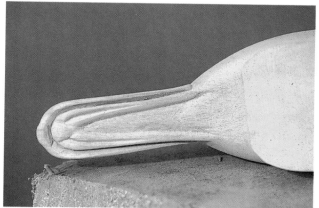

The underside of the bill. The lamellae will be defined using a sharp-pointed burning tip

Close-up of bill detail

2   The widest point of the head is marked*. Note that from* into the bill is almost a straight line. If it is too curved it will look as if the duck is puffing its cheeks out.

3   The bill. On most dabbling ducks such as Mallard, Pintail, Teal and Gadwall, the bill has more or less parallel sides. A very common mistake is to point the bill. If anything, it may be slightly narrower at the head end (see illustration above left.).

The best way to get the bill correct in every detail, is to use a 'study bill'. These indispensable aids to carving are resin castings taken from the bill of a freshly killed duck, before shrinkage has occurred. The bills of taxidermy mounts invariably suffer from shrinkage, so giving a misleading shape and size if used as reference material. By using callipers and a study bill, it is possible to get the bill of your carved duck exactly the right shape and size.

A number of ducks have highly individual bills, e.g., the Shoveler and Red Breasted Merganser, so it is important to use a study bill to help you to get the correct shape.

4   The upper and lower mandibles separate when the duck quacks. It is the lower mandible that hinges when the bill opens – the upper is to all intents and purposes fixed in relation to the skull. Using a study bill also makes the carving of the underside of the bill easier.

5   The position of the eye is a very critical factor in

TOP: *The head is ready to be glued to the body. A wood dowel, or in this case, a steel dowel screw is used to strengthen the glue joint. Fast-setting epoxy glue is used, as it is convenient and very strong*

giving your duck the correct expression. If the eyes are too far forward the duck will look aggressive, if too high it will look very aloof and so on. Use photographs and reference material and your own observation to figure out where the correct position of the eye should be in relation, say, to the top rear point of the bill. Then use a glass eye of the appropriate size and see how the expression changes on your pattern, as the eye position is varied. Try to find the position which looks best. The eye is certainly the most important feature of the head. We always engage eye to eye with people and animals and it is important, therefore, to give your duck a realistic expression. Always use the best quality glass eyes. It is pointless to spend days carving a beautiful duck, then to spoil it with a cheap eye which ruins the effect. Generally, in a duck like the Mallard, the eyes should be spaced slightly farther apart than the width of the bill. Again, use your reference material.

When ready, the head is glued to the body, using five-minute epoxy glue. Glue is spread on both surfaces, then the head is positioned by pressing the two pieces of wood together and holding firmly until the glue sets. As soon as the glue has hardened, the shaping of the neck area is completed. Then, finally, the whole duck is thoroughly sanded until smooth.

Feather texturing is achieved mechanically, using various burrs and grinding stones, or by burning with an electrically heated feather burning tool or a combination of both. If you examine a feather, you will note several important things. The quill is

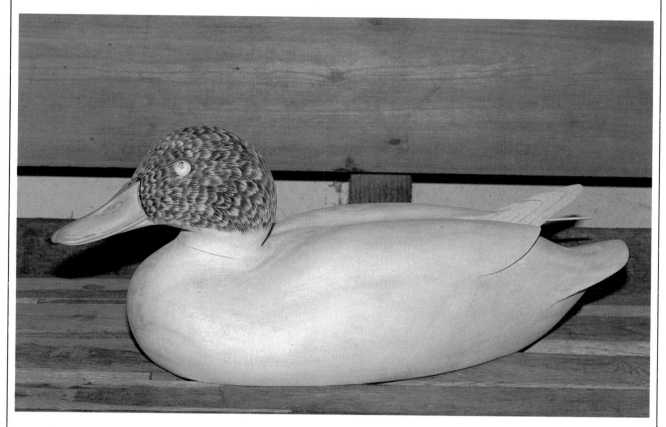

curved. The barbs are also curved and lie at a fairly shallow angle to the quill. Avoid straight lines if you want your duck to look soft and feathery. Small feathers have quills but they are so fine that they need not be represented separately.

The electrically heated tools used for feather burning range from the inexpensive type fitted with a single shape tip (which can be replaced when worn) and no heat control; to very sophisticated − and more expensive − equipment, with a wide range of tips, giving great versatility and fineness. An excellent feather burner for the beginner is the Hot Tool, which does a good job and is very dependable.

A feather burner is a burning tool, not a cutting tool. Most beginners are inclined to be too heavy-handed and to burn too deeply. It is wise to practise on pieces of scrap wood to start with, to get the feel of the tool before you start on your duck.

A duck has different types of feathers in different areas of its body. The extremely fine feathers of the head give the appearance of hair − it is difficult to distinguish individual feathers. By contrast the wing feathers, especially the primaries and tertials, are large feathers; the primaries have to be very strong to give the drive necessary to propel the bird in flight. These feathers have the quill close to the leading edge; this helps to create the right aerodynamic shape for lift and manoeuvrability. When you observe live ducks, study the feathers closely and note all the different types and sizes. It is advisable to mark in pencil the feathers to be burned. 'Feather flow' is important, that is, all the feathers must flow

ABOVE: *The feather burning tool being used to texture the head*

TOP: *The head has been glued on and the neck area must now be shaped and sanded*

*The feather texturing defines individual feathers and must
be done with care and patience. The better the feather
texturing, the easier it will be to paint the duck later*

along the body and wings in a streamlined way; if you think of the bird in flight, this is obvious.

Feather texturing is best done sitting in a very comfortable position, holding the duck in such a way that you can work easily and holding the tool like a pen. Don't rush. The trick is to move at an even rate so that the texture is uniform in depth. You can check that you are achieving texture by testing for a 'washboard' effect. If you run a fingernail across your feathers, you will be able to feel and hear the texture like a fine washboard.

Feather texturing, using a burner, takes time and patience. It can be very satisfying and with patient practice good results can soon be achieved.

There are several flexible drive machines popular with duck carvers; my own favourite is the American Pfingst machine which has a ⅛ HP motor. It can be fitted with several types of hand pieces to enable different types of rasps and burrs to be used. It has a foot-operated speed controller and has a range of 2000 to 14000 rpm. Using Karbide Kutzell rasps, wood can be removed at an impressive rate. Finer

burrs and tips, such as ruby carvers and diamond cutters are ideal for a variety of shaping and texturing jobs.

Mechanical tools may be noisy and dusty but they save a considerable amount of time and some excellent results may be achieved with them. Again, remember to protect yourself from dust and eye damage.

In carving a realistic style decorative decoy, we have to decide how to deal with primary feathers, which in dabbling ducks stick out well clear of the body. They can be carved from the solid block: this calls for considerable carving skill and patience. Alternatively, and commonly, they are made as separate inserts and for a beginner, this is a simpler method. The primary feathers emerge from beneath the large tertial feathers, so we cut a thin slot beneath these feathers to receive the primary inserts. These in turn, are cut out of a thin sheet of wood and fitted to the slot. When a snug fit is achieved, the inserts can be feather textured. A similar procedure is adopted for the Mallard tail curl, which is usually

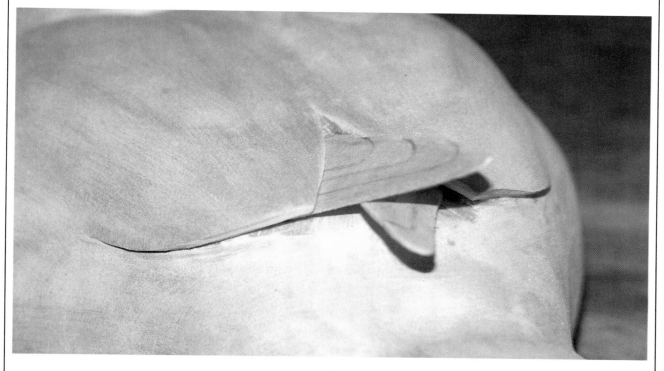

carved separately and glued into a small hollow, shaped to receive it.

With the carving and texturing finished, the wood is now sealed, prior to painting. A very fine sealer from a spray can, Krylon 1301 or 1302, gives good results. Alternatively, use a shellac sanding sealer. We make sure it is brushed well into the surface, as we want to be sure that the whole duck is sealed. The trick is to brush it on generously and then brush it out finely. It is important to avoid clogging the fine texture that we have been to so much trouble to achieve in the feather texturing stage. Once sealed, the duck is ready for painting.

The primary feather inserts are located in the slots beneath the tertial feathers. They are fitted by trial and error until they are a firm fit. After the painting they will be glued into place

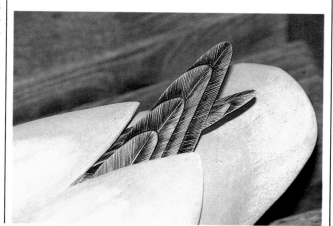

... AND PAINTED

Ready to paint. Painting demands concentration, the right materials and a dust free environment. Here a sheet of polythene has been laid out on a table and will serve as a palette for mixing the colours. Note the modified 6" diameter potter's wheel being used as a turntable. This greatly facilitates the painting process. The plastic bucket contains plenty of water for washing brushes and the hair dryer will be used to accelerate the drying of the acrylic paint

ecorative decoys can be painted either with acrylic paints or oil paints. Most carvers use acrylic because it dries quickly and is easy to use.

In simple terms, paint consists of two components, solid and liquid. The solid is the colour pigment, the liquid is the vehicle in which it is suspended, enabling it to be spread easily over the object being painted. The liquid then evaporates leaving the dry colour evenly dispersed.

A feather looks like a feather because of the way it reflects light. The feather texture we have applied to the carving simulates the light/shade reflection of the feather. Seen in section our texture is shown in the illustration on p.181.

In the painting stage we have to preserve this light reflective texture. We must avoid filling the texture with thick paint thereby reducing its reflectiveness.

What we have to do, then, to keep the texture well defined, is to apply the paint in thin washes, that is, a little solid in a lot of liquid. If we use acrylic paint, we simply thin down the paint from the tube with water and apply the paint wash by wash, depositing a small amount of colour with each pass. Each wash has to dry thoroughly and this can be accelerated using a hair dryer, holding it far enough away to avoid blowing the paint up into waves.

This is a time consuming process but it produces excellent results when done well. Acrylic paint applied thickly finishes up with a *shine*; what we hope to achieve is a *sheen*, the same sort of sheen that real feathers have. Most experts agree that a fine coat

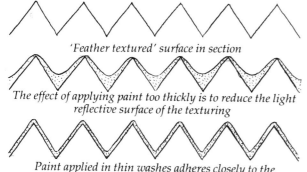

'Feather textured' surface in section

The effect of applying paint too thickly is to reduce the light reflective surface of the texturing

Paint applied in thin washes adheres closely to the texturing to give a crisp texture with a fine 'sheen'

The duck was first sealed before painting then a well watered down coat of gesso applied. This serves as a primer and helps to absorb some of the glossiness of the acrylic paint

of gesso, well watered down, applied over the sealer, helps to absorb some of the glossiness of the paint and gives the surface something artists call 'tooth', helping the paint to grip the surface better. Gesso is available in acrylic form, so it is completely compatible with the colour paints.

Now that we have some idea of the process, we have to work out where the colours go. This is where your research pays off. You should have made notes of the colours of the duck and I recommend making a colour chart before you start painting on the duck. This can be along the same lines as painting by numbers. Draw your duck and paint in the colours, making a note of the various mixes. If you are completely new to painting, you will have to become familiar with all the colours available. Ducks are wonderfully colourful creatures, yet most of their colours are the so-called earth colours, made of fine ground earth and rock substances. These may appear quite dull in themselves but when applied will produce wonderfully rich colourful results.

The most commonly used colours in bird painting are these: –

Titanium white	Pthalo green (dark green)
Ivory black	Pthalo light green (emerald)
Burnt umber	Violet
Raw umber	Indian red
Burnt sienna	Crimson
Raw sienna	
Yellow ochre	
Ultramarine blue	

*Using very thin washes of acrylic paints, the basic colours
are sketched in. The density of colour is then slowly built up
with a succession of thin washes, care being taken to dry
thoroughly between each wash*

With these colours it should be possible to paint any duck, either drakes and ducks (hens). You will also need some acrylic glazing medium and iridescent powders. You will have noticed a number of ducks have bright iridescent colouring on their feathers. The head of the mallard drake is a fine example of this brilliant colour effect. It is virtually impossible to reproduce this exactly with paints to the extent it is in nature, because it is the physical construction of the feather that produces the spectacular changes of colour. Yet a remarkably satisfactory effect can be achieved using iridescent powders, which can be applied with the paint to give your duck as much realism as possible. There are various ways of applying iridescent powders. Perhaps the most satisfactory way for beginners is to

sprinkle the powder into a 30/70 mixture of acrylic glazing medium and water. Stir the powder in, then apply as a thin glaze in the areas where the iridescence occurs. A word of warning — a little iridescence goes a long way — apply it sparingly for best results. Too much and your duck will look gaudy and cheap.

Colour blending is an important part of decorative decoy painting. The transition from one colour to another in certain areas has to be achieved as smoothly as possible. This is certainly something that takes plenty of practice. Try this simple exercise in wet blending. Take a piece of plain brown cardboard from a box and seal with sanding sealer. Allow to dry. This surface will correspond closely to that of wood. Mix any two colours, say pale grey and burnt umber, to a consistency of single cream. With a wash brush,

The head of a Mallard drake has a brilliant iridescent sheen.
The application of a thin glaze containing iridescent powder
adds this finishing touch to the carving

apply the grey paint across the top of an area about four inches deep and burnt umber across the bottom, so that the colours meet midway, edge to edge. Do this swiftly so that the two colours stay wet. Wet blending can obviously only be done if both colours are still wet. Now clean and quicky 'blot dry' the brush on absorbent kitchen roll paper. Now with the almost dry brush work along the interface of the two colours. This will give you a colour mix at the interface, a mid brown colour. Now quickly clean and blot dry the brush again. Now continue to work along the edges of the blend area, gradually losing any hard edges until you have a smooth transition from burnt umber to grey with no obvious point of change. Now observe the large tertial feathers on the back of a drake Mallard. Get the idea? Keep practising and you

will soon become confident and able to work swiftly. The secret of success is to work *along* the join — not across — and to keep cleaning and drying the brush. You may, if you wish, use several dry brushes to save time. There are some excellent special blending brushes available.

A word here about brushes. Paint brushes are expensive; good ones are very expensive. Therefore, you should treat them with respect to get the best out of them. Always wash brushes the moment you have finished using them. If you have to answer the 'phone, drop your brush into water (if using acrylics) to keep it from drying out. Acrylics dry rapidly and if the paint is allowed to dry in the brush you will have difficulty cleaning it and its shape may well be ruined. When cleaning the brush do so in plenty of

A basic set of brushes like these will enable you to make a good job of painting your duck. Always buy the best brushes you can afford and take good care of them

(a) *Wash brush*
(b) *General purpose brush*
(c) *Fine detail brush. Best sable*
(d) *Very fine detail brush, used mainly for vermiculations*
(e) *Special feather edging brush. Hand made in finest sable*

Colour blending is an important part of decorative decoy painting technique. Try an exercise like this, on a sheet of sealed cardboard, for practice

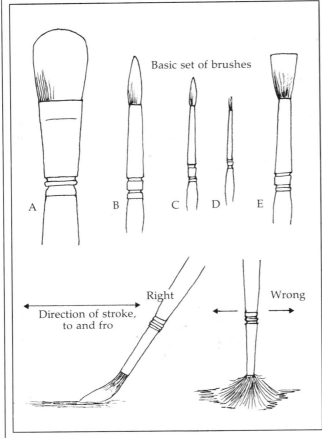

Basic set of brushes

A B C D E

Right

Wrong

Direction of stroke, to and fro

clean water; a bucketful is best. Move the brush rapidly to and fro to wash out the paint, lightly flick off any excess water, then gently blot the dry brush on absorbent kitchen roll paper. Shape the hairs lightly into shape — some people do this in their lips — then lay the brush flat to dry. Never dry by squeezing and pulling the hairs between the fingers; if you do you will soon be irritated by loose hairs in the paint as you work.

Take my advice and buy the best brushes you can afford, look after them well and never lend them to other people. To start with you will need the following brushes: –

A fine detail brush   A feather edging brush
A wash brush
A no. 7 size general purpose brush

There are many different styles of brushes all designed to do different jobs. Add to your basic kit as you try new types of brush. Never mix paint with a brush, always use a palette knife. Plastic ones are very cheap and it pays to have two or three.

As already mentioned, have a bucket of water for cleaning your brushes and a smaller vessel containing clean water for mixing colours and thinning down paint. A drinking straw or spoon can be used for lifting water out onto the palette. For a palette, try using builder's polythene sheet which can be thrown away when you have finished painting. You can place a sheet of white paper beneath it to give you a good background against which to judge colours.

When painting ducks, I always use a heavy steel potter's turntable, with the table reduced in radius to 6″. This, with a cork bathroom tile glued to the top surface to avoid slipping, makes an ideal way to get around the duck easily without having to handle it all the time.

Another aspect of duck painting that calls for practice is vermiculation. Vermiculations are small wormlike wavy lines that are to be found on many duck feathers. They may be quite noticeable, as on the back of a Scaup drake or very subtle, as on the side pocket feathers of a Mallard drake. Find a few duck feathers and study the vermiculations on them. You will find that the lines stop and start in a very random way yet the overall effect is quite uniform. Vermiculations on your carvings can be done with a very fine paint brush using watered down acrylic paint of

*With practice and patience your efforts will be rewarded
with a decorative decoy that will give you immense
satisfaction*

appropriate colour. Certain very fine felt-tipped pens are suitable but only if the ink is permanent — otherwise the ink would smudge if handled. When painting vermiculations, try to develop a slight shake with your hand as you go to get the right sort of wavy line. Study your reference material and practise. In no time at all you will have mastered it.

It is usual when painting a duck to paint over the eye. This saves going carefully around it with the many thin washes that have to be applied. When you have finally finished the painting the magic moment of cleaning off the eye arrives. Using your fingernail to avoid scratching the glass, start at the outside edge of the eye and peel off the paint which comes away easily. If you find that the paint tears away slightly at the edge of the eye, you can touch in carefully with

paint to make good.

Now your duck is finished and looking back at you as you stand back to admire your handiwork.

Just one more thing. How about the underside of the duck? It is interesting to note that people will always want to pick up your duck and the first thing they do is turn it over and look at the underneath. No one knows exactly why this is, but believe me, it happens. So be sure to sand the base of your carving and maybe apply a coat or two of clear lacquer to show the wood. Some people paint the base. I always think this is hiding the wonderful material that everyone loves — wood. Let people see that you have carved this work of art from wood. And finally, don't forget to sign and date your work.

Persevere and good carving!

BIBLIOGRAPHY

AMERICAN BIRD DECOYS, William J. Mackey Jr., (USA) Schiffer, 1965

AMERICAN DECOYS; From 1865 to 1920, Quintina Colio (USA) Science, 1972

AMERICAN FACTORY DECOYS, Henry A. Fleckenstein Jr. (USA) Schiffer, 1981

AMERICAN WILDFOWL DECOYS, Jeff Waingrow (USA) Dutton, 1985

ANATOMY OF A WATERFOWL, Charles W. Frank Jr. (USA) Pelican, 1985

BIRDS OF PREY – Blue Ribbon Techniques, William Veasey (USA) Shiffer, 1986

CARVING MINIATURE WILDFOWL, With Bob Guge & Roger Schroeder (USA) Stackpole, 198?

CHAMPIONSHIP CARVING, Tricia Veasey & Tom Johnson (USA) Schiffer, 1984

CHAMPIONSHIP WATERFOWL PATTERNS – Volume 1, Lifesize Studies of North American Marsh Ducks, Patrick Godin (Canada) Godin Art Inc., 1986

CHAMPIONSHIP WATERFOWL PATTERNS – Volume 2, Lifesize Studies of North American Diving Ducks, Patrick Godin (Canada) Godin Art Inc., 1987

CONNECTICUT DECOYS, Henry C. Chitwood (USA) Schiffer, 1987

DECOYS: A North American Survey, Gene & Linda Kangas (USA) Hillcrest, 1983

DECOYS: The Art of the Wooden Bird, Richard LeMaster (USA) Contemporary, 1982

DECOYS OF MARITIME CANADA, Dale & Gary Guyette (USA) Shiffer, 1983

DECOYS OF THE MID ATLANTIC REGION, Henry A. Fleckenstein (USA) Schiffer, 1979

DECOYS OF THE MISSISSIPPI FLYWAY, Alan Haid (USA) Shiffer, 1981

FACTORY DECOYS OF MASON, STEVENS, DODGE & PETERSON John and Shirley Delph (USA) Schiffer, 1980

FLOATERS AND STICK-UPS, George Reiger & Kenneth Garrett (USA) Godine, 1986

FLOATING SCULPTURE: The Decoys of the Delaware River, H. Harrison Huster with Doug Knight (USA) Hillcrest, 1983

GAME BIRD CARVING, Bruce Burk (USA) Winchester, 1972

HOW TO CARVE WILDFOWL, Roger Schroeder (USA) Stackpole, 1984

HOW TO CARVE WILDFOWL Book 2, Roger Schroeder (USA) Stackpole, 1986

'L.T. WARD & BRO – Wildfowl Counterfeiters' in *North American Decoys*, Byron Cheever (ed.) (USA) Hillcrest, 1971

NEW ENGLAND DECOYS, John & Shirley Delph (USA) Schiffer, 1981

NEW JERSEY DECOYS, Henry A. Fleckenstein Jr. (USA) Schiffer, 1983

SHANG: *A biography of Charles E. Wheeler*, Dixon MacD. Merkt with Mark H. Lytle (USA) Hillcrest, 1984

SHOREBIRD DECOYS, Henry A. Fleckenstein Jr. (USA) Schiffer, 1980

SONGBIRD CARVING, Rosalyn Daisey & Sian Pat Kurman (USA) Schiffer, 1986

SONGBIRD CARVING II, Rosalyn Daisey & Sina Pat Kurman (USA) Schiffer, 1987

SONGBIRD CARVING WITH ERNEST MUEHLMATT, Roger Schroeder (USA)

Stackpole, 1988

SOUTHERN DECOYS OF VIRGINIA AND THE
CAROLINAS, Henry A. Fleckenstein Jr. (USA)
Schiffer, 1983

THE ART OF BIRD CARVING, Wendell Gilley
(USA) Hillcrest, 1972

THE ART OF THE DECOY, Adele Ernest (USA)
Schiffer, 1982

THE FISH DECOY, Art, Brad & Scott Kimball
(USA) Aardvark, 1986

THE FISH DECOY II, Art, Brad & Scott Kimball
(USA) Aardvark, 1987

THE GREAT GALLERY OF DUCKS, Richard
LeMaster (USA) Contemporary, 1985

THE HISTORY OF BOROUGH FEN DECOY, Tony
Cook & R.E.M. Pilcher (UK) Providence, 1982

THE MAKING OF HUNTING DECOYS, William
Veasey (USA) Schiffer, 1986

THE STORY OF LEM WARD, As told by Ida Ward
Linton to Glen Lawson (USA) Schiffer, 1984

TUNNICLIFFE'S BIRDS, C.F. Tunnicliffe (UK)
Gollancz, 1984

WATERFOWL CARVING: Blue Ribbon
Techniques, William Veasey (USA) Schiffer,
1982

WATERFOWL CARVING WITH J.D. SPRANKLE,
Roger Schroeder, J.D. Sprankle (USA)
Stackpole, 1985

WATERFOWL DECOYS OF SOUTHWESTERN
ONTARIO, R. Paul Brisco (USA) Boston Mills,
1986

WATERFOWL PAINTING: Blue Ribbon
Techniques, William Veasey (USA) Schiffer,
1983

WATERFOWL PATTERNS & PAINTING, Jim
Sprankle (USA) Greenwing, 1986

WATERFOWL: The Artist's Guide to Anatomy,
Attitude & Color, Richard LeMaster (USA)
Contemporary, 1983

WETLAND HERITAGE: The Louisiana Duck
Decoy, Charles W. Frank Jr. (USA) Pelican,
1985

WILD FOWL DECOYS, Joel Barber (USA) Dover,
1934

WILDLIFE IN WOOD, Richard LeMaster (USA)
Contemporary, 1978

WILDLIFE WOODCARVERS, Chapell & Sullivan
(USA) Stackpole, 1986

USEFUL ADDRESSES

MUSEUMS

Havre de Grace Decoy Museum,
P.O. Box A,
Havre de Grace,
MD 21078,
USA

The North American Wildfowl Art Museum,
Salisbury State College,
Salisbury,
MD 21801,
USA

The Peabody Museum,
Salem,
Massachusetts,
USA

The Refuge Waterfowl Museum,
Maddox Avenue,
Chincoteague,
Virginia,
USA

Shelburne Museum,
Shelburne,
Vermont,
USA

Note: Some of these museums are closed during winter months and on certain days of the week. You are advised to check opening times with the museum before planning a visit.

AUCTION HOUSES

James Julia/Gary Guyette Inc.,
Dept H, RFD 1, Box 830,
Fairfield, ME 04937,
USA

Richard A. Bourne Co. Inc.,
P.O. Box 141,
Hyannis Port,
MA 02647
USA

Richard W. Oliver Auction Gallery,
P.O. Box 337, Kennebunk,
Maine 04072,
USA

OTHER USEFUL ADDRESSES

The Decoy Gallery,
Kingshill,
Chewton Mendip,
Near Bath,
Somerset,
BA3 4PD
England

A comprehensive range of other decoy books, together with The Wallchart of British Waterfowl by Hilary Burn, may be obtained from The Decoy Gallery.

School of Decorative Decoy Carving,
Decoy Art Studio,
Farrington Gurney,
Bristol, Avon,
BS18 5TX
England

Information service and six-monthly newsletter. Decoy carving courses and mail order carving supplies and books.

INDEX